John Milton's *Paradise Lost*

Reading Guides to Long Poems

Published:
John Milton's Paradise Lost: *A Reading Guide*
Noam Reisner
Hbk: 978 0 7486 3999 1
Pbk: 978 0 7486 4000 3

Edmund Spenser's The Faerie Queene: *A Reading Guide*
Andrew Zurcher
Hbk: 978 0 7486 3956 4
Pbk: 978 0 7486 3957 1

Homer's Odyssey: *A Reading Guide*
Henry Power
Hbk: 978 0 7486 4110 9
Pbk: 978 0 7486 4109 3

Forthcoming:
Elizabeth Barrett Browning's Aurora Leigh: *A Reading Guide*
Michele Martinez
Hbk: 978 0 7486 3971 7
Pbk: 978 0 7486 3972 4

Alfred Lord Tennyson's In Memoriam: *A Reading Guide*
Anna Barton
Hbk: 978 0 7486 4135 2
Pbk: 978 0 7486 4134 5

John Milton's *Paradise Lost*
A Reading Guide

Noam Reisner

Edinburgh University Press

Edinburgh University Press Ltd
22 George Square, Edinburgh

www.euppublishing.com

Typeset in 10.5/13 Sabon
by Servis Filmsetting Ltd, Stockport, Cheshire, and
printed and bound in Great Britain by
CPI Antony Rowe, Chippenham and Eastbourne

A CIP record for this book is available from the British Library

ISBN 978 0 7486 3999 1 (hardback)
ISBN 978 0 7486 4000 3 (paperback)

Contents

Preface

Paradise Lost rewards a lifetime of reading and re-reading, but it is also a daunting poem which initially can disorient and alienate first-time readers. Among long narrative poems, *Paradise Lost* is certainly one of the longest and most intimidating in the English canon. Many students are daunted not only by the sheer length of the epic, but also by the perceived 'heaviness' of the theological and biblical subject matter, the sprawling baroque artificiality of the poetry, Milton's ostentatious pedantry and classicism, and his Latinate syntax and difficult idiom. As a consequence, it is a common schoolroom practice to ease students into the epic by breaking it up into discrete units, usually focusing first on the most pleasing aspects of the poem for modern readers – namely Satan's vividly realised character in the early books and the captivating story of Adam and Eve's fall from God in the Garden of Eden in Books IX and X. As a result, many important sequences in the poem deemed by popular consensus (and even some critical opinion) too difficult or of inferior poetic quality are often neglected or even ignored, with the obvious result of sabotaging the proper coherence of Milton's overall didactic argument in the poem. The following *Reading Guide* to *Paradise Lost* approaches the perceived problem of the poem's length by offering first-time readers and students a detailed analytical overview, or map, of the poem as a whole, together with a corresponding map for negotiating important landmarks in the vast body of academic criticism on the poem. The two sets of maps are inseparable; the various critical debates which surround different aspects of the poem raise a set of very useful, and usually insoluble, questions which in turn crystallise, through the heated debates they inspire, the poem's unique claims on our imagination. The analyses and discussions provided in this *Guide* are representative rather than exhaustive and aim to demonstrate the wide scope of interpretation *Paradise Lost* invites. To grasp Milton's vision in its complex totality and to engage with the demanding questions it poses about the fallen human condition requires from the reader both patience and constant attention to detail. The main aim of this *Guide* is to alert readers to the complex interpretative choices the poem demands of them, and to provide a basic set of tools with which to approach these acts of interpretation by situating Milton's great epic historically and intellectually in its time, and exploring some of its major themes as they emerge from these contexts.

In writing this *Guide* I have incurred many particular as well as more general debts to former teachers, present colleagues and numerous students. Although the emphases and syntheses in the materials of this *Guide* and some of the more discrete observations are my own, what follows is above all a tribute to the monumental scholarship and insight of the poem's modern editors and the cumulative efforts of a wide community of Milton scholars who in their diverse body of work best embody the sheer range of interpretation the poem continues to excite. Although it is not possible to acknowledge all such debts individually in such a *Guide*, the vast majority of my scholarly debts are recorded in the annotated bibliography in Chapter 4. From a more personal perspective, I wish to register my enduring gratitude: to my teachers John Carey and the late A. D. Nuttall, who made my initial encounter with *Paradise Lost* a more forgiving and fascinating experience than it might have been; to Colin Burrow for his continued advice and support; and to Sally Bushell who trusted me with this project and saw it through with diligence and a great generosity of spirit. I would also like to acknowledge my research assistants on this project, Ron Ben-Tovim and Olga Barenboim, who between them transcribed and proofread many of the passages from the poem reproduced in this *Guide*. Miss Barenboim also acted as a keen student reader, making many helpful suggestions. And last but not least, this *Guide* is primarily indebted to my students in two different universities and two very different countries who taught me much as we ventured together across the Miltonic gulf of chaos – this *Guide* is for them.

In transcribing passages from the poem I have relied on the lightly modernised edited text of the poem prepared by John Leonard for his Penguin Classics edition. I wish to thank Penguin Classics for giving me permission to replicate a substantial amount of this text for the purpose of analysis and discussion. It is recommended that students who wish to read this *Guide* alongside the poem itself do so with reference to this edition (for more on different editions of the poem see the bibliography). In writing this *Guide* the following conventions have been observed: all quotations from the Bible are from the Authorised Version. Full biblio-graphical details are given in notes only to those items not listed in the annotated bibliography (Chapter 4) while items so listed are given in short title form. All references to Milton's prose are to *The Complete Prose Works of John Milton*, 8 vols, general ed. Don M. Wolfe (New Haven, CT, and London: Yale University Press, 1953–1980), henceforth designated with the abbreviation *CPW*. All references to Milton's poetry other than *Paradise Lost* are to *John Milton: The Complete Poems*, ed. John Leonard (London: Penguin Classics, 1998).

Series Editors' Preface

The form of the long poem has been of fundamental importance to literary studies from the time of Homer onwards. The *Reading Guides to Long Poems* series seeks to celebrate and explore this form in all its diversity across a range of authors and periods. Major poetic works – *The Odyssey, The Faerie Queene, Paradise Lost, The Prelude, In Memoriam, The Waste Land* – emerge as defining expressions of the culture which produced them. One of the main aims of the series is to make contemporary readers aware of the importance of the long poem for our literary and national heritage.

How 'long' is a long poem? In 'The Philosophy of Composition' Edgar Allan Poe asserted that there is 'a distinct limit, as regards length, to all works of literary art – the limit of a single sitting'. Defined against this, a long poem must be one which *exceeds* the limit of a single sitting, requiring sustained attention over a considerable period of time for its full appreciation. However, the concept of poetic length is not simply concerned with the number of lines in a poem, or the time it takes to read it. In 'From Poe to Valéry' T. S. Eliot defends poetic length on the grounds that 'it is only in a poem of some length that a variety of moods can be expressed . . . These parts can form a whole more than the sum of the parts; a whole such that the pleasure we derive from the reading of any part is enhanced by our grasp of the whole.' Along with Eliot, the series editors believe that poetic length creates a unique space for a varied play of meaning and tone, action and reflection that results in particular kinds of reading and interpretation not possible for shorter works. The *Reading Guides* are therefore concerned with communicating the pleasure and enjoyment of engaging with the form in a range of ways – focusing on particular episodes, tracing out patterns of poetic imagery, exploring form, reading and re-reading the text – in order to allow the reader to experience the multiple interpretative layers that the long poem holds within it. We also believe that a self-awareness about *how* we read the long poem may help to provide the modern reader with a necessary fresh perspective upon the genre.

The *Reading Guides to Long Poems* series will engage with major works in new and innovative ways in order to revitalise the form of the long poem for a new generation. The series will present shorter 'long poems' in their entirety, while the longest are represented by a careful selection of essential parts. Long poems have often been read aloud, imitated or even translated in excerpts, so there is good precedent for appreciating them through selective reading. Nevertheless, it is to be hoped that readers will use the *Guides* alongside an appreciation of the work in its entirety or, if they have not previously done so, go on to read the whole poem.

Ultimately the Edinburgh *Reading Guides to Long Poems* series seeks to be of lasting value to the discipline of literary studies by revitalising a form which is in danger of being marginalised by the current curriculum but is central to our understanding of our own literature, history and culture.

Sally Bushell with Isobel Armstrong and Colin Burrow

Chapter 1
Mapping and Making *Paradise Lost*

Historical engagement

For all its timeless, universal qualities, *Paradise Lost* is also a product of its time, or, to be more accurate, the product of one man's extraordinary English Protestant imagination at work *in* its time. Uniquely for a poem which now enjoys a high canonical status, *Paradise Lost* remains fundamentally a national English Protestant epic born of the political and religious upheavals of the seventeenth century and addressed, as the invocation to Book VII indicates, to a 'fit audience . . . though few' (31) of like-minded Protestant revolutionary readers who have presumably suffered and lost with Milton in the cause of liberty and religious non-conformity. Although its poet assumes the mantle of universal prophecy, the epic situates its abstract theological and philosophical ideas in the vicissitudes of rebellion and conflict, as played out in a very specific point in time, within a specifically English political–historical narrative of civil war, regicide and the precarious English dream of a republican commonwealth. The biblical myth of the 'Fall' – that is, the account in Chapter 3 of Genesis of Adam and Eve's loss of paradise – was for Milton in this respect not some remote *aete*, or cause, for all human sinfulness, but an event of calamitous moral and spiritual error which mankind has slavishly repeated throughout its fallen history, and will probably continue to do so until the Second Coming when 'one greater man' shall 'Restore us, and regain the blissful seat' (I. 4–5).

In Milton's eyes, the failure of the English revolution and the republican enterprise which followed the civil war between the forces of Parliament and Charles I was just another chapter in the triumph of tyranny over human weakness. 'Tyranny' took for Milton many forms. It was to be found and resisted with any man-made law, institution or person in a position of power who oppressed in any way the individual

Reformed Christian's spiritual and civic liberties, but he also thought of it in more abstract terms as an evil force in the world synonymous with ignorance, irrationality, and idolatry which in his view often led to such oppression to begin with. The spiritual struggle between liberty and tyranny is the single most consistent principle behind Milton's political and ideological commitments, and it also forms the main subject of much of his poetry as well. In *Paradise Lost* especially, it is the conceptual axis around which the epic poetry gravitates, forcing the reader to reassess continually, rather than flatly accept, the timeless ideas the poem otherwise interrogates. In order to have a better sense of this dynamic process at the heart of the poem it helps, therefore, to understand something about the historical forces which shaped Milton's imaginative engagement with his subject.

The John Milton who came to write *Paradise Lost* was a radical revolutionary in the full sense of the term, in his poetry, politics and religious ideology, but he was not always so. As the recent biography of Milton by Gordon Campbell and Thomas N. Corns shows (see the bibliography in Chapter 4), Milton's radicalism must be understood as a process which led him from the doubts and open curiosity of childhood to the highly ambivalent and complex perspectives of old age. The doubts and curiosity of his youth always shaped Milton's scholarly approach to the world, but after the traumatic events of the civil war and his own life experiences in its shadow, the innocence was gone and with it a willingness to compromise. Milton was not born a radical revolutionary, he became one, one might say, almost despite himself. Born in 1608 and raised up in a devout, but highly cultured, Protestant household, Milton lived through and participated in some of the most tumultuous decades in English history. His lifetime spanned the rise of Laudianism in the English Church and the Personal Rule of Charles I, the civil war and the defeated king's unprecedented trial and execution outside the Palace of Whitehall on 30 January 1649, the subsequent creation of the republican Commonwealth and Cromwell's Protectorate, and the final breakdown of the republican regime and the Restoration of the monarchy in 1660. Throughout his life, Milton never stood by as history unfolded around him – he staked his claim in shaping it. Whether as an independent pamphleteer, as the secretary for foreign tongues for Cromwell's Council of State, or as a self-styled poet-prophet, Milton always took an active interest in what he perceived to be his bounden Christian duty to help reform and mould the English Church and state, and defend the Reformed Christian's inalienable right to pursue and defend liberty, whether in England or abroad.

It is in this spirit that for twenty years, roughly 1640 to 1660, Milton put aside his major poetic endeavours and launched himself into the public arena against the background of the civil war and an emerging republic as a pamphleteer and polemicist, staking his domestic and international reputation as a defender of regicide and the English republican cause. This period of frantic political activity produced some of the most memorable works of polemical prose in the English language, most famous of which today are the still relevant and inspiring attack on state censorship of the press in *Areopagitica* (1644), and such influential manifestos of Christian-humanist republicanism as the *Ready and Easy Way to Establish a Free Commonwealth*, published on the eve of the Restoration in 1660.

Milton's growing sense of disillusionment with temporal politics took several decades to develop and was attendant in fact on a number of deeply unsettling national and personal crises. As a young man in the early 1640s, for example, Milton allied himself unequivocally with the Presbyterian cause against the rule of the bishops in the English Church, but following the abolition of the Carolinian episcopacy in 1643, when Presbyterianism was adopted by the Long Parliament as the official alternative model for governance of the Church, Milton soon found that here too schism was inevitable given the threat to individual liberties posed by the new, allegedly reformed regime. In 1643, the Westminster Assembly of Divines set out to impose a rigid Presbyterian model on all English churches, but ultimately met fierce resistance from the growing faction of Independents with whom Milton increasingly sympathised. The Independents, who enjoyed Cromwell's patronage and wide support from the army, resisted any attempt to impose fixed modes of worship and confessional conformity on a national scale. With 'liberty of conscience' as their rallying call of reform, Independents like Milton argued that each parish and congregation should have full scope to elect its leaders and determine its religious practices and confessional positions without the oversight of a central, governing body. Milton in fact took an even more radical stance on these matters, consistently insisting that it was up to individual reformed Christians to worship according to their conscience. He famously registered his disgust with the encroaching tyranny of the Westminster Assembly in a political poem he composed towards the end of the so-called 'second civil war' in 1646, 'On the New Forces of Conscience under the Long Parliament', which concludes with the famous line: 'New *Presbyter* is but old *Priest* writ large'.

It is important to remember, however, that the classically educated, humanist Milton was never a 'puritan' in the conventional sense, either in his theology (as we shall see below) or in his psychology. He was certainly not raised as a puritan as many often suppose. The mature Milton saw himself as a man apart, ordained by God to achieve great things in divinely inspired poetry, and it is as a would-be poet-prophet that he finally approached the world in the hope of correcting its ills. While Milton indeed baulked from the dogmatism of the Presbyters, as a committed rationalist with a clear sense of his self-worth as a cultivated poet and scholar he also had little sympathy for the growing phenomenon of religious enthusiasm and mysticism which took root in many of the proliferating radical sects thriving under the banner of 'liberty of conscience'. Just as he had no patience for overbearing potentates in Church and state, Milton had nothing but contempt for mobs of uneducated, uncultivated zealots whose iconoclastic agendas he thought of as barbaric. For Milton, being an Independent in political and ecclesiastical matters increasingly came to mean being alone, even when he could agree with, or draw inspiration from, the spiritual or political ideas of this or that sectarian group on the religious fringe of English society. The result was a contradiction: while in some of his polemical tracts, for example in *Areopagitica* or the much later *Of True Religion*, Milton defended freedom of conscience and the many different religious confessional positions it gave rise to as necessary for liberty, he also hoped naively that such a free exchange of ideas would allow for a supreme truth to emerge which any rational, conscientious Christian should be able to see for themselves and agree on. When this failed, when all that emerged was discord, Milton tended to retreat defensively into his church of one, guarding his projected persona's integrity from what he refers to allusively in *Paradise Lost* as 'the barbarous dissonance / Of Bacchus and his revellers' (VII. 32–3). The allusion here is to the myth of Orpheus, the archetypal poet and singer, with whom Milton often identified in his writings. Just as Orpheus, who could move stones with his music, was finally torn to pieces by the frenzied handmaidens of Bacchus for preferring the rational, refined music of Apollo to the raucous, emotive music of the wine god, so Milton feared that his singular claim to fame as a cultivated child of the Muses would be drowned out amid the cacophony of dissenting radicals bent on nothing but political as well as spiritual anarchy.

Matters came to a head following Cromwell's death on 3 September 1658, when what little order and organisation there was under the republican government quickly fell apart. It was now becoming abundantly clear even to the idealist Milton, still in the service of the government, that the dream of an ideal English republican commonwealth of educated, freethinking Christians was melting away before the grim realities of petty politics, greed for power, religious intolerance and crippling schism. Tyranny was once again rearing its head everywhere. No suitable republican leader could be found to fill the massive personal vacuum Cromwell had left behind; the republican camp fell into political disarray; and the royalists were on the ascendancy. Milton, having probably begun work on *Paradise Lost*, nevertheless once again very courageously and recklessly threw his efforts into polemical prose in an attempt to restate the principles of radical Christian and political liberties he believed the English republic should be founded on. It was to no avail. As calls to restore the monarchy increased, Milton's sense of embittered isolation became more extreme, as did his contempt for the English people's slavish degeneracy in willingly subjecting themselves to what he bravely called on the eve of the Restoration the 'detested thraldom of kingship'[1] – it was the Fall of Adam and Eve all over again.

Following the Restoration of the monarchy in 1660, for reasons which are not entirely clear, Milton the notorious regicide escaped the scaffold and unlike many of his revolutionary friends was only briefly imprisoned. His public and literary republican persona, on the other hand, was less fortunate. On 27 August 1660 Milton had to endure the news that a hangman in London was publicly burning his indexed books by order of the king. These were years of isolation, financial difficulty, slander and constant danger for the long-since blind and now ageing Milton. These were also the years when, withdrawn from public affairs but never from the spirit of public engagement, he composed with the assistance of family, friends and amanuenses the majority of *Paradise Lost*. The clearly autobiographical lines invoking Urania, the heavenly muse, in the opening of Book VII of the epic paint a striking picture of Milton's sense at the time of his isolation, but also of his sense of privileged prophetic vocation, as he imagines the muse of direct divine inspiration visiting him nightly, dictating to him lines of the poem:

> Standing on earth, not rapt above the pole,
> More safe I sing with mortal voice, unchanged
> To hoarse or mute, though fall'n on evil days,
> On evil days though fall'n, and evil tongues;
> In darkness, and with dangers compassed round,
> And solitude; yet not alone, while thou
> Visit'st my slumbers nightly, or when Morn
> Purples the east: still govern thou my song,
> Urania, and fit audience find, though few.
> (VII. 23–31)

A sense of political, personal, and finally intellectual solitude and loss created then the imaginative conditions which gave birth to *Paradise Lost*. All of Milton's gifts as poet, polemicist, scholar, teacher and thinker came together in a poetic creation alive with his polemical instincts and rhetorical flair, but also with his tremendous sympathy as an educator and a deep abstract thinker. The result is a poem that reaches to heaven and hell and all that stretches between them, but which remains forever rooted in the very English earth of politics, ideology and conflict from which it grew.

Conceptual outline

Milton poured into *Paradise Lost* a lifetime of learning and thinking on a wide range of theological, philosophical and political questions. The poem also reflects his range of scholarly interests in astronomy, history, logic, law, mathematics, music, the New World and travel narratives, and the natural created world, God's so-called 'book of nature'. As it is impossible to do justice to all of these conceptual dimensions of *Paradise Lost* in the scope of such a short introductory survey, readers are encouraged to consult the annotated bibliography for further reading and the text and commentary section of this *Guide* to gain some sense of the complex range of Milton's thought as it is reflected in the poem. Nevertheless, coming to terms with some of the key ideas Milton explores poetically in *Paradise Lost* is necessary to gain a deeper appreciation of the poem's intellectual complexity, and what follows is a brief outline of these.

It should always be remembered that Milton was not a rigorous or even original theologian, philosopher or political thinker as far as the ideas themselves are concerned. He was, however, highly original and independent in the poetic and narrative synthesis of the numerous, often irreconcilable ideas deployed in the service of his 'great argument' (I. 24) in *Paradise Lost*. Moreover, Milton's thinking was always evolving, and he tended to adjust his positions and views on key questions depending on the context and the period in his life, so that using Milton's earlier prose, for example, to illuminate ideas in *Paradise Lost* can be a treacherous enterprise. Be that as it may, we know what Milton thought about most of the burning issues of his day, especially in theology, thanks in large part to a prose Latin manuscript known as *De Doctrina Christiana* (*On Christian Doctrine*), now thought to be undoubtedly the work of Milton. The manuscript in question is a systematic theological treatise dating probably from the late 1650s. The treatise sets out a rather unorthodox Protestant theology (but hardly as heretical or unusual as has often been supposed), especially notable for its views on creation being *ex Deo* (from God) rather than *ex nihilo* (from nothing), its mortalism (the idea that the soul dies with the body), and a Christology which rejects traditional Trinitarian theology as an unbiblical scholastic innovation. Some echoes and connections between ideas explored in the treatise and *Paradise Lost*, especially on the Trinity, the atonement and creationism, seem unmistakable. Because, however, *De Doctrina* and *Paradise Lost* are two very different texts, composed in very different genres and with very different aims in mind, it is reckless to draw simple correlations between them. Consequently, with one small exception later on, I shall not be referring in this survey or indeed in the commentary sections of this *Guide* directly to the theology of *De Doctrina*, but only to ideas as they are relevant to, and find expression in the poem.[2]

The intellectual make-up of *Paradise Lost* is best understood in the context of the combined Protestant-spiritual and humanist-scholarly traditions in which Milton was educated and which shaped his thinking. The two traditions often overlapped in Milton's England and complemented each other, but not always harmoniously. As a committed Protestant, Milton believed that it was up to each individual Christian to read the Bible for themselves, especially in matters pertaining to individual justification through faith and final salvation. Like all Protestants, he held that the Bible, and especially the New Testament, was written by the prophets and apostles through the direct inspiration of the Holy Spirit and that the resulting text contained the purest, unadulterated divine truth testifying to the New Covenant under Christ between fallen humanity and God. However, whereas Calvinists (who represented the dominant strand of Protestant faith in Milton's England) believed that a reader's ability to interiorise the Bible's one true spiritual sense was a revelatory function of superimposed grace illuminating the passive reader, Milton always championed the active agency of educated, informed readers. As a devoted humanist believing in the inalienable dignity of man's rational faculties, Milton departed therefore from mainstream Calvinism in significant ways. For Milton, reason was a divine gift not to be squandered and its free exercise in spiritual matters ennobled and lifted fallen man from his sinful imperfections. Controversially for a Protestant writing in a predominantly Calvinist milieu, therefore, Milton rarely, if ever, acknowledged directly his own sense of sinfulness as most puritans tended to do, and always insisted that the sort of inner illumination Calvinists and other more radical Protestants lay claim to should be translated into rational and literary cogency.

Milton saw himself as heir not just to the intellectual legacy of the Genevan Reformation, therefore, but also to the Italian Renaissance's optimistic philosophy of man which talked of each individual as a unique, morally accountable microcosm at the centre of God's creation. According to this broadly Neoplatonic, mildly Christian scheme, man has a choice either actively to embrace through learning his created divinity as a rational being and so rise to the height of the angelic intelligences, or forfeit this divine birthright, becoming a slave to sensual appetite and barbarity. This tradition placed special emphasis on the role of 'right reason' (*recta ratio*) in education and nurture as a remedy against fallen nature, and promoted in this respect the role of morally edifying poetry to move men to virtue. Sir Philip Sidney's influential *Defence of Poesie*, an Elizabethan treatise arguing for the moral value of poetry, belongs to this tradition, as does Milton's blatantly heretical project of theodicy in *Paradise Lost*, where he not only claims to 'assert Eternal providence', but also to 'justify the ways of God to men' (I. 25–6).

The term 'theodicy', first coined by the philosopher Leibniz in the early eighteenth century, is a neologism deriving from a combination of the Greek words for 'God' (*theos*) and 'justice' (*dike*). It alludes to any attempt to explain the logic of theological ideas, usually the presence of evil in the world, based not on revealed religious 'truth' and articles of faith, but only by reflecting analytically on God's immanent activity in the world through his works of creation. Put in more simple terms, *theodicy*, or what is otherwise termed 'natural theology', seeks to address major theological questions through a rational analysis of the available evidence in Scripture and the world at large. It is clear, then, why Milton's audacious project of justification more or less falls into this category. In rejecting traditional Protestant ideas of irresistible revelation and trying to work out rationally and logically through the study of Scripture and human history the theological truths he believed in, Milton of *Paradise Lost* is indeed something of an early modern natural theologian. Although he strongly believed in the idea of Adam and Eve's original sin and its devastating inherited implications on all of fallen humanity, Milton also believed that man may, through learning and education, better himself en route to regaining 'A paradise within thee, happier far' (*Paradise Lost*, XII. 587). This process, moreover, depended for Milton precisely on dynamic acts of reading which call on the reader not just to interpret the text, but to continually reassess the nature of the interpretative act itself in the pursuit of an abstract idea of 'truth', that like a Platonic ideal always drives the interpretative process, even as it finally eludes it.

Out of this basic synthesis between Protestant and humanist views on man's place in creation and his moral and spiritual agency grew Milton's many other correspondingly distinctive ideas, namely his monism, Arminianism, Christology, antinomianism, and republicanism. The following is a brief survey of each of these.

Monism

The most important idea for an understanding of the poetics of *Paradise Lost* is Milton's belief that the entire created universe, and man especially, is part of a unified material continuum, where spirit (soul) and matter (body) are relative degrees rather than opposites, and where all created beings aspire to return to the single perfection and material unity of the one true God. Angels, for example, are distinctly material beings in *Paradise Lost*. They have an active metabolism and can apparently feel pain and suffer wounds, but their bodies consist of such rarefied matter that they can assume any form they wish and act in all other respects as beings of pure spirit. Since spirit and matter are one substance in this scheme, extending from God in increasingly less attenuated form, Milton's monism is sometimes called more technically 'animist materialism' (the belief that the whole universe consists of single matter in different degrees of inspirited animation), or alternatively 'animist monism' (the term used in this *Guide*), 'monistic materialism', and other possible combinations of these terms. Whatever one calls it, Milton's monism extends from his belief, recorded also in *De Doctrina*, that God created the world not out of nothing (that would be illogical and unscriptural according to Milton), but by creating first a chaos of raw matter drawn out of God himself, from which God then created everything else in the universe. While several important extra-biblical sources, such as Plato's *Symposium* and the *Timaeus*, and Lucretius' classical philosophical epic *On the Nature of Things*, contributed to Milton's monistic thinking, the resulting monism of his poetry is not just philosophical but also theological and Pauline in character. Milton's animist monism can be explained almost entirely with reference to his reading of the Pauline Epistles, especially Romans and 1 and 2 Corinthians. It extends from his deep familiarity with the Pauline Epistles' discussion of fallen humanity as embodied creatures, where the rational soul is not trapped in a body, but rather is itself embodied as a measure of it being *in* the world created by God. The famous Pauline dichotomy between a life lived according to the spirit and a life lived according to the flesh represents in this scheme two radically opposed modes of existence which implicate the entire embodied creature – body and soul – either in a spiritual life which brings one closer to God, or a sinful, idolatrous life lived in denial of God. Part of the confusion about this sort of monistic anthropology is that on either extreme of the continuum, where one extreme is God himself and the other is corrupt, sinful matter, the monistic paradigm does seem to collapse into dualistic distinctions which trap the created human being between two moral and spiritual existential dimensions. But it is precisely the ethical core of Milton's monism that the movement on this Pauline axis between a life lived *according to* (rather than in) the flesh and a life lived *according to* the spirit calls on man to exercise freely his rational moral judgement in obedience to the spirit, rather than the letter, of God's Word. This principle governs Milton's belief in the need to seek for unity through diversity in all things, and goes a long way to explain the perceived unevenness of hierarchical relation-ships in *Paradise Lost*, where the subordination of the Son to the Father, or of Eve to Adam, imply finally monistic unity rather than dualistic opposition.

Arminianism

In defending the importance of free will in his theology of original sin and the atonement, Milton placed himself outside the Lutheran–Calvinist consensus of his time, siding in effect with a minority position within the Calvinist landscape loosely labelled as 'Arminian', after the teachings of the influential Dutch reformer Jacobus Arminius (1560–1609). Arminianism, as set out formally in the Remonstrance of its adherents in 1610, challenged Calvinist theology chiefly on the question of predestination. The argument was essentially about the goodness and power of God. For Calvin and his English heirs God could only be said to be 'good' in a predicative analogical sense, whereas his unconstrained power was an essential and absolute attribute. Calvin reasoned that if God is truly omnipotent, omniscient, infinite and eternal (as he has to be if he is God), it necessarily followed that his decrees, as recorded in Scripture, are above the constraints of time and causality and therefore irrevocably absolute. This led Calvin to develop the theory, almost by way of logical necessity, that if you truly believe in God's omnipo-tence it must follow that God, foreknowing that man will fall, decreed outside created time that a small portion of humanity will be saved, while the rest will perish in damnation. The resulting theory of so-called 'supralapsarian double predestination' (that is, God predestining all men either to damnation or election before the Fall) was not in fact the most central idea in Calvin's theology, but in its absolute denial of human free will and its insistence on the complete corruption of fallen man by sin it resulted in devastating psychological implications. All that a man or a woman could do in this unforgiving Calvinist scheme was hope that they were among those 'elected' for salvation and so behave accordingly, not that they might gain anything by acting virtuously, but, strange as it might sound, in order to demonstrate to themselves and others that they *have been* elected. The result was a potentially crippling psychological state of mind prone to deep anxiety and despair, famously captured, for example, in the writings of John Bunyan, where the sinner constantly struggles to discover signs and assurances of his or her state of grace and election.

Arminius and his followers, among them evidently Milton, stridently objected to this despairing theology, and were willing to compromise on God's absolute omnipotence to salvage his fundamental goodness. Arminians argued that God in his goodness and love delegated power to his creatures by giving them free will, and that this free will is entirely consistent with God's eternal and omnipotent majesty. Moreover, they denied that for God to foreknow is to foreordain, argued that with the exception of the decree of free will what Calvin called divine decrees were actually conditional promises, and rejected as unbiblical Calvin's theory of double predestination. This led to a corresponding argument about the nature of grace, since the Arminians, stressing the importance of free will in human salvation, rejected the related Calvinist notion that Christ died on the cross only for the elect and that the gift of God's grace to the elect must be therefore irresistible. Arminians conceded that grace was 'prevenient', that is, that grace was a gift of God's mercy that always preceded any act of faith, but they maintained that it was up to the individual believer to either reject or accept this gift of 'prevenient' grace. In the eyes of the Arminians, and Milton as well, 'election' was therefore conditional and merited rather than predestined and imputed, while damnation and reprobation were correspondingly seen as not consequent on any divine decree at all, but simply as due punishment for wilfully rejecting God's gift of grace. Milton was exposed to Arminian ideas as a student at Cambridge and probably at home as well, and although he must have disliked the way in which Arminian theology was later hijacked by the right-wing politics of High Churchmanship and episcopacy, by the time he came to write *Paradise Lost* he had openly embraced most of its key teachings. As we shall see in the commentary sections, the Arminian theology of free will, or something very close to it, is central to Milton's theodicy in *Paradise Lost*, even as it battles it out with a residual Calvinist celebration of God's inscrutable majesty and power. It accounts for how Milton presents the idea of the Fall in the poem and God's justice towards Adam and Eve, as well as the essential quality of prayer and repentance after the Fall, where, aided by 'Prevenient grace' (XI. 3), a regenerated Adam and Eve are reconciled to the hope of fallen humanity's eventual and never irresistible salvation through the mercy and sacrifice of the Son.

Christology

The Son in *Paradise Lost* intercedes on behalf of fallen humanity and offers to atone for Adam and Eve's sin. As a theological idea this is entirely orthodox, but when such an abstract idea is translated into the dramatised action of an epic narrative something odd happens to the theology. How Milton understood the role of the Son in the theological scheme of *Paradise Lost* is yet another area where he seems to have held a highly unusual minority position within the Reformed spiritual landscape. Milton's independent reading in Scripture led him to question the nature of the Holy Trinity and the relationship of its persons. However, whereas the *De Doctrina Christiana* manuscript is explicitly and stridently anti-Trinitarian, *Paradise Lost* is only circumstantially so. Many passages in the poem usually interpreted as representing an anti-Trinitarian position (where the Son is distinct from but not necessarily inferior to the Father) can also be read in rhetorical terms of more abstract subordination that may be reconciled after some straining, if not with orthodox Trinitarian theology, then certainly with the meagre biblical proof texts Church Fathers have always appealed to in defending the idea of one God who is three. After all, both the Father and the Son are called 'God' in the poem, and the dramatic interaction between them as *characters* could well be simply a dramatisation through epic narrative of a theology which identifies the harshness of the Father's justice and the intercession of the Son's mercy as two distinct but never mutually exclusive aspects of a unified Godhead. Moreover, the relationship between the Father and the Son appears to be not one of strict subordination, but of the Son functioning as a 'Divine similitude' (III. 384) of the Father, implying perhaps that the Son is a projection or extension of the Father's will rather than a categorically inferior created being. Nevertheless, elsewhere in the poem it does seem as if some form of distinctly unorthodox anti-Trinitarianism creeps into the narrative presentation of the theology. What may have begun as a literary exercise in rationalising and dramatising the complexity of divine unity, as opposed to a strictly scholastic Triune unity, does end up presenting in the poem a literally paternal relationship between the Father and the Son which suggests clear subordination of a son to his father. The most damning evidence in this respect is the clear indication that the Father begets the Son at a specific moment in time, therefore implying that the Son, unlike the Father, is not eternal. Indeed the Son's actions in the poem seem to follow a similarly subordinated causality within narrative time. It is the Son, as a distinct narrative character rather than merely a theological persona, who at a given moment volunteers to redeem man from under the wrath of the all foreknowing Father, and it is the Son who as the Messiah straps on his father's sword and rides a chariot into battle against the rebel angels in heaven, as his father sits back and watches the inevitable and rather comical carnage of immortal angels entering non-mortal combat. Whatever the theological conclusions one wishes to draw from such passages, one gets the feeling that what is at stake here is finally a literary question about the representation of God in the poem and only incidentally about theology. The distinction between the Son as an extension or the instrument of God's will in time is a very fine one and in theological terms it could easily be interpreted as a mark either of unity or of subordination. In fact, interested readers might wish to consider here the paradoxical possibility of subordinated unity. Either way, however, the vision of deity that ultimately emerges from the poem in its entirety is unified and remarkably consistent and it depends, as always with Milton's monism, on relative distinctions and diversity within a monistic filial hierarchy, rather than on simple Unitarian or pantheist abstractions.

Antinomianism

Antinomianism, from the Greek for 'against' (*anti*) and 'law' (*nomos*), is a mostly pejorative theological term first coined by Martin Luther after the Reformation. It refers to the belief current especially in some strands of Protestantism that the gift of divine grace frees Christians from having to observe not just the ceremonial Mosaic law (that is, the various legalistic religious observances given to the Jews under the law of Moses), but the moral law implicit in the Ten Commandments as well. Luther coined the term to single out and warn against those Protestants who took his teachings on justification by faith alone (*sola fide*) to disturbing, lawless extremes. The antinomians Luther was worried about took a very radical view of the liberating power of divine grace after the coming of Christ, resting their theology on a reading (many will say a gross misreading) of key Pauline passages alluding to the complete liberty from the law under the Christian dispensation, for example in Romans 7: 5–6:

> For when we were in the flesh, the motions of sins, which were by the law, did work in our members to bring forth fruit unto death. But now we are delivered from the law, that being dead wherein we were held; that we should serve in newness of spirit, and not in the oldness of the letter.

Pauline liberation theology is very complex but it has at its heart a basic principle which holds that Christians are accountable before God not to the letter of any temporal law, moral or otherwise, but to the *spirit* of the moral law as it is inscribed in the hearts of believers through the gift of grace. The problem with this idea, as Luther soon discovered, is that it is possible to take this theology to mean that since the letter of the law is so fundamentally opposed to the spirit, no Christian is bound to any temporal law whatsoever even morally, resulting therefore in very peculiar beliefs in the indifference of carnal or bodily licentiousness to a life of the spirit.

The phenomenon of antinomianism predates in fact the Lutheran Reformation. The early Gnostics were often accused of being antinomians and Paul himself evidently fended off similar accusations from his legalistic opponents by consistently reminding his addressees in his Epistles that Christ came to fulfil the law, not to destroy it. As Romans 3: 8, for example, indicates, Paul was particularly horrified at the implication some have been 'slanderously' drawing from his teachings that it is permissible to do evil so 'that good may come'. For Paul, complete liberty from the law of sin under Christ entails a far deeper moral and spiritual responsibility. This was, after all, the implication to be drawn directly from ideas already contained in Christ's Sermon on the Mount, which famously rephrases the Ten Commandments to make them more, not less, demanding morally, for example in Matthew 5: 27–8:

> Ye have heard that it was said by them of old time, Thou shalt not commit adultery: But I say unto you, That whosoever looketh on a woman to lust after her hath committed adultery with her already in his heart.

As 'antinomian' was a term of abuse, few Christians ever openly confessed themselves to hold such views, though many were accused by others of holding them. For his part, Milton was a vocal antinomian in many of his prose writings, but of a conservative Pauline disposition. Milton followed Paul very carefully in distinguishing between the law under Moses (ceremonial as well as moral) which Christ fully abrogated, and God's law of the spirit which is absolutely binding and rigorous. Christian liberty for Milton was never, therefore, to be confused with irrational, idolatrous licence and unexamined human autonomy. Consequently, Milton never allowed the argument for anti-nomian freedom to translate into open-ended liberty of conscience and tolerance for all, but only for those who could merit such liberty based on what Milton considered, rather vaguely, a rational interpretation of Scripture according to a 'sound Protestant maxim'.[3] What is relevant to *Paradise Lost* therefore is the way in which Milton often deploys on the one hand antinomian concepts in political debates about temporal and religious liberty within the state, but on the other hand talks of the need strictly to obey the law of God imparted to the individual believer as a precondition of liberty itself. For Milton this is never a contradic-tion, but a basic principle of rationalised Pauline Reformed theology. These beliefs probably developed early on from Milton's attacks on the Carolinian episcopacy, fuelling his political stance as an Independent and his belief that Reformed Christians, as long as they approached the words of Scripture logically and rationally, were free to worship according to their conscience without being bound to any temporal law, liturgy or confession. This qualified and very guarded form of rational antinomianism provides an important link between Milton's theology and his politics, and as we will see in the next chapter, it lies at the heart of Milton's project of theodicy in *Paradise Lost* as well.

Republicanism

As mentioned above, all of Milton's more abstract philosophical and theological ideas in *Paradise Lost* extend finally from his search for unity in all things and his emerging animist monism. The principle of an active heuristic drive towards an ever elusive yet present unity also shaped Milton's abstract political views, and offers the important link between his philosophical theology and his republican ideology. Milton's belief in the need for a unified vision of 'truth' won through debate and trial in the court of logic and right reason (rather than a court of mere uninformed public opinion) also accounts for his political stance as an Independent who defended the English republic against the tyrannical abuses of monarchy. Here too, however, as with the theology and philosophy, the reader of *Paradise Lost* is presented with a difficult question of interpretation. In his polemical prose, Milton was deeply committed to engage with contemporary political questions about sovereignty, tyranny, liberty and the merits of a free Christian commonwealth, but he did so within the confines of the polemical genres in which he was writing, and in a very specific historical context which led him to espouse a set of views relevant only to *that* given context. For example, when Milton defended the execution of the king and attacked the abuses of the Stuart monarchy he never once attacked the institution of monarchy as such, but rather the tyrannical abuse of such a sacred biblical institution by specific individuals. Equally, when Milton drew on his classical learning to defend very abstract republican values in the idea of a free commonwealth, he did so not as an ardent constitutional republican but because that was the best model for the government of England at that time in the absence of a just, God-fearing king who would serve his people rather than rule them. The exercise of setting out an ideal republican model was mostly confined, therefore, to speculative definitions and not the drawing out of intricate constitutional practice. Like many other republican writers at the time, Milton was finding that he was called upon as an apologist for the new regime first and foremost to supply English politics with a republican vocabulary with which to make sense of the chaotic political situation the English state was thrust into after the fact of the king's execution.

Milton's republicanism was classical in nature and reactionary in practice. His notion of a free commonwealth rested on an amalgam of classical and Pauline notions of liberty, where a body-politic or common-wealth was defined by its ability to govern itself and provide for the well-being of its members without the tyranny of a single individual or a foreign power interfering in its affairs. The way to promote such well-being was through informed debate, where no authority remained unchallenged, and where the resulting flexibility ensured that the political executive could always adjust to shifting circumstances in meeting these goals. Atrophy and stasis, therefore, were the bane of good governance in Milton's view; no form of government and no constitutional arrangement, including a republic, were of any value if they were not themselves always open to criticism and reform by their own members acting in concert to maintain the integrity of proactive liberty in the commonwealth. As a consequence, Milton did not favour by definition this or that form of government within the broadly defined parameters of a republic; what mattered to him – at least as it comes across in his political writings after 1649 – was that no government would lapse into tyranny where it served its own interests rather than the overall well-being of its people. Milton, however, was no democrat. Aristotle's famous saying in his *Politics* that 'They should rule who are able to rule best' runs as a thread of guarded elitism through all of Milton's political thinking. In *Paradise Lost* 'the popular vote' (II. 313) is confined to the devils' abortive democracy in hell, while in his final major poem, *Paradise Regained*, Milton has Jesus himself voicing similar contempt for the common sort of people, whom Jesus describes as a 'herd confused, / A miscellaneous rabble, who extol / Things vulgar' (III. 49–51). Milton was probably horrified at the idea of a radical, popular democracy and believed that a free commonwealth should be governed only by an intellectual meritocracy of educated and therefore virtuous Christian citizens sharing power democratically. It is this principle of dynamic liberty secured by the few for the many, founded largely on Ciceronian humanist ideals of education and civic responsibility and the Pauline ideal of absolute Christian freedom from the abrogated Mosaic law, which animates much of the seemingly abstract theology in *Paradise Lost*. It is the conceptual engine which drives the didactic engagement of the poem with its intended 'fit . . . though few' readers, where no perspective is left unexamined and no theory untested in the process of defending a comprehensive vision of divine justice and providence at work in the fallen world.

Creative development and style

Nothing is known for certain about the order in which the blind Milton dictated and assembled the books of the epic, or about his numerous likely revisions of sections read back to him. However, we do know far more than we usually do for any author from this period about the creative development which led Milton to write his great epic. Drafts and fragments preserved in Milton's notebook, written mostly during the 1630s and early 1640s and now known as the Trinity Manuscript, indicate that Milton had toyed with the idea of a poem on the biblical story of the Fall for some time before the plan for the epic poem we now possess matured. Perhaps because he felt as yet unready to undertake the project of an epic poem, the younger Milton of the 1630s initially envisioned staking his claim to poetic fame by writing a dramatic poem, or play, partly based on the allegorical morality tradition, partly drawing on the formality and pathos of Greek tragedy. The manuscript contains in Milton's hand a long list of possible topics on which he was thinking to write such a poem, including numerous biblical stories as well as themes and narratives drawn from British history. Significantly, the manuscript also contains several rough drafts or outlines for a tragedy, or dramatic poem, on the biblical story of the Fall entitled 'Paradise

Lost' in its third draft, but then renamed in the fourth, more developed outline, 'Adam Unparadized'. The drafts list names of characters, sketch out very briefly a few speeches (for example a prologue spoken by Moses) and draw a rough outline of the possible plot which, as the title of 'Adam Unparadized' suggests, centres mostly on the temptation of Adam and Eve in the garden and subsequent loss of paradise.[4]

We will never know why Milton eventually abandoned his plan for a dramatic poem on the Fall in favour of epic. It is possible that as he matured and the subject grew in his mind he realised that the enormity of the story would be better served by the narrative scope of epic. However, while Milton undoubtedly had a classically informed and elevated view of the epic genre, he does not appear to have pursued consistently or even seriously the so-called Virgilian 'rota' of creative development, progressing from pastoral, through didactic georgics to epic, in quite the same way as did, for example, his Elizabethan predecessor Edmund Spenser. Milton instead continually tested his poetic ability and refined his lyrical voice in different genres, so that when the intellectual and biographical circumstances were ripe to tackle finally the great poetic project he believed himself destined to compose, the diffused material of his earlier work came together in an astounding synthesis. Any theory or speculation about Milton's choice of genre and artistic decision regarding *Paradise Lost* is therefore weakened by the sheer complexity of the poem Milton ended up composing. Many different elements, such as the use of allegory and dramatic insets, as well as pastoral tableaus, lyrical elaborations and georgic digressions, all combine with the more traditional elements of epic subject matter and tonality to form in *Paradise Lost* a multifaceted, and by no means monolithic, baroque epic universe, where various forms of poetic representation and narrative techniques compete and complicate each other.

Milton's drive towards unity through diversity, which as we noted is a major thematic preoccupation of his philosophical and theological outlook, is also reflected in his multilingual English which unifies and subsumes into its idiom a wide range of linguistic registers assimilated over years of scholarship and wide reading in ancient as well as modern European languages. The mature Milton's literary and linguistic scope was immense. His mastery of Latin could rival the greatest classicists of his age; he had solid command of Greek and most likely of Hebrew as well (though to what extent he could actually read Hebrew is still debated); and he was fluent in both French and especially Italian, in which he composed as a young man several elegant love sonnets. Milton read widely and experimented poetically in all of the languages available to him. From classical poetry, he drew special inspiration from the prosody and generic conventions of Virgil, Horace and Ovid which in his youth he imitated in a series of very accomplished Latin elegies and lyric poems. In drama, to which he was always attracted, Milton especially admired the Greek tragedies of Euripides and was well versed in the legacies of Elizabethan and Jacobean theatre, in particular of the great masters Marlowe, Jonson and Shakespeare, to whose respective poetic styles Milton owed a profound creative debt. Milton also had a voracious appetite for the flourishing continental, mostly Italian and neo-Latin literature of the high Renaissance, and was patently inspired by the Christian epic tradition inaugurated by Dante and developed in the Renaissance most notably by Du Bartas in France and Tasso in Italy. However, above all else, Milton's imagination, language and mature style were steeped in the Bible, which he could read just as fluently in the original Greek (and possibly even in Hebrew for the Old Testament) but which he mostly remembered in large sections learnt by heart in the Latin translation of the sixteenth-century Jewish convert to Christianity, the Protestant humanist Immanuel Tremellius. The Bible was to Milton a source not just of spiritual inspiration, but of artistic and generic inspiration as well. As a devout, literary-minded Protestant, Milton believed that the Bible contained the finest models of any genre, either in tragedy (the Book of Job), lyric poetry (the Psalms) or epic (the Old Testament history books). The classics and contemporary literature shaped Milton's imagination and suggested to him poetic forms, conventions and themes, but the Bible shaped his thinking on every possible topic, as well as his distinctive sense of prophetic, not to say apostolic poetic authority.

Milton's multilingualism and wide reading, weighted heavily towards Latin literature, accounts therefore for the baroque ornateness, idiom and the syntactical flexibility of his English verse form in *Paradise Lost*. While today Milton's English poetry is widely acknowledged as only inferior perhaps to Shakespeare (and here too it is a matter of drawing fine distinctions), this was not always so. The objection to Milton's mature English style, especially in *Paradise Lost*, was formulated in the eighteenth century and reached its apogee with the negative criticism of F. R. Leavis and T. S. Eliot in the first half of the twentieth century. Eliot is especially famous for opining that Milton's imposing influence on later generations of English poets did 'damage to the English language from which it has not wholly recovered'.[5] Eliot in particular objected to the alleged unnaturalness of Milton's English, and his tendency to drown images and concepts in aural embellishments that create superfluously magniloquent sound effects divorced from the main idea of a given sentence. The so-called 'Milton controversy', which saw C. S. Lewis and William Empson defending Milton against this criticism (from very different perspectives), was decidedly won in Milton's favour by Christopher Ricks, who in his now definitive study, *Milton's Grand Style*, demonstrated that Milton was capable of far more subtlety and precision than his detractors of over two centuries ever allowed. Since then, Thomas N. Corns, John Leonard and John K. Hale, in a number of different studies (see bibliography), have completed the picture, elucidating the complex nature of Milton's baroque English.

While the Latinity of Milton's idiom and its alleged unnaturalness have probably been exaggerated, Milton's English is nevertheless undeniably remote from the rhythms and idioms of spoken English, especially today. However, the reader needs to distinguish between historical remoteness and purposeful loftiness arising from generic decorum. Milton's English was much less remote in the seventeenth century than it is today, but even then it tended to move away from demotic expression towards more formal or scholarly English which naturally (though not always) relied on Latin phrasing and constructions. The overriding principle of Milton's English in *Paradise Lost* is not, however, one of deliberate grandeur or anti-demotic elitism (though these views of Milton's style are not uncommon), but of poetic diction covering a very wide range of registers always self-referencing its wrought nature as art. In *Paradise Lost*, the idiom, musicality and elegance of Spenser, Shakespeare and Jonson combine with Latinate, Italianate and Hebraic constructions and turns of phrase to produce a lofty, carefully crafted style of almost plastic qualities, with a near limitless, rhetorically sophisticated expressive range.

The metre of *Paradise Lost* is iambic blank verse, almost without exception in lines of ten syllables (decasyllables), usually ending with a strong monosyllabic stress. The opening line of the poem is typical of the overall structure but also of its flexibility (stressed syllables are in capitals): 'Of | MAN'S | FIRST | dis|ob|ED|ience|, AND | the | FRUIT'. As the trochee of the second stress already indicates, individual lines may vary tremendously in metrical patterns, creating a sense of immense freedom beyond the simple rigidity of the standard iambic pentameter tread.[6] In any case, this was certainly not the accepted metrical style for heroic or epic English verse at the time. Blank verse was almost entirely confined to the stage, and never before exhibited such extravagances in the length and complexity of sentences. At the time, the established metre for epic or formal poetry was either rhymed stanzas or heroic couplets, of which

John Dryden, a Restoration contemporary of Milton, was the supreme master before Alexander Pope perfected the form (though Dryden too eventually abandoned rhyme later in life for blank verse). As with anything else, Milton relished the opportunity this singularity gave him to set himself apart as a radical dissenting from what he believed was a hopelessly decadent and slavish Restoration culture. Milton seized on the political metaphor his rejection of rhyme offered him, and added to the 1668 reprint of the first edition of *Paradise Lost* a spirited prefatory defence of his verse form which politicises the matter. Milton's tone in the preface is uncompromising: 'The measure is English heroic verse without rhyme, as that of Homer in Greek, and of Virgil in Latin; rhyme being . . . the invention of a barbarous age, to set off wretched matter and lame metre'. Moreover, in composing his poem without rhyme, Milton insists that he has no less than liberated English verse from degenerate slavery:

> This neglect then of rhyme so little is to be taken for a defect, though it may seem so perhaps to vulgar readers, that it rather is to be esteemed an example set, the first in English, of ancient liberty recovered to heroic poem from the troublesome and modern bondage of rhyming.

This swipe at Dryden and his contemporaries is more than just witty banter; it is in fact deeply revealing about the close link in *Paradise Lost* between the poem's style and its religious-political content, where ideology translates into prosody. Milton replaced the binding rigidity of the rhymed couplet with an innovative verse form which is indeed much freer and intellectually demanding than anything else composed at the time, and then linked the resulting form to the poem's central argument about liberty on a deep aesthetic and thematic level.

If idiom and prosody elevate *Paradise Lost* and set it apart aesthetically, it is the poem's complex syntax which holds the frame together and gives the poem its relentless sense of action and movement. When reflecting on syntax in *Paradise Lost* it is important to remember that Milton was an expert prose polemicist. From his Cambridge days as a disputant, Milton honed the skill of debating in Latin a topic on either side of the argument, and was especially adept, it seems, at playing the 'devil's advocate'. The ability to use elaborate rhetorical devices to present as persuasive the partisan logic of an argument he himself believed to be patently false accounts for much of Milton's instincts as a polemicist in later years, where his ability to discredit an opponent by reversing their own argument against them was unsurpassable for its time. When Milton composed *Paradise Lost*, many of the rhetorical habits he acquired in his years as a polemicist came into play poetically, resulting in long, complex sentences with many subordinate clauses requiring from the reader a great deal of mental agility and alertness. Milton is especially fond of Latinate syntactical constructions where the key verb is suspended until the end of a long sentence, allowing ideas to develop in stages for greater effect, often with many surprising twists and turns along the way. Here, for example, is the opening sentence of the poem which extends over sixteen uninterrupted lines of verse:

> Of man's first disobedience, and the fruit
> Of that forbidden tree, whose mortal taste
> Brought death into the world, and all our woe,
> With loss of Eden, till one greater man
> Restore us, and regain the blissful seat,
> Sing Heav'nly Muse, that on the secret top
> Of Oreb, or of Sinai, didst inspire
> That shepherd, who first taught the chosen seed,
> In the beginning how the heav'ns and earth
> Rose out of Chaos: or if Sion hill
> Delight thee more, and Siloa's brook that flowed
> Fast by the oracle of God; I thence
> Invoke thy aid to my advent'rous song,
> That with no middle flight intends to soar
> Above th' Aonian mount, while it pursues
> Things unattempted yet in prose or rhyme.
> (I. 1–16)

The key verb here is 'sing', but it is delayed until the sixth line, while the rest of the sentence qualifies in a number of dependent clauses the Muse whose singing the poet is enlisting. The first half of the sentence thus introduces the subject of the poem, putting great stress on the key word 'disobedience', while the second half of the sentence asserts and qualifies the poet's prophetic authority in a rising yet equivocating movement which mirrors the idea of soaring with no 'middle flight' but which also captures something of the anxiety attending such audacity. This syntactical strategy, replicated in many different patterns throughout the poem and combined with the occasional short, powerful sentence interjected for more dramatic effect, allows for the supreme control of the argument. It also accounts for the extraordinarily varied affective impact different passages of the poem can have on the attentive reader.

Syntax, lineation and prosody in *Paradise Lost* always track each other in complex patterns that defy the rigidity of stop ended lines, typical for example of much dramatic blank verse (but not Shakespeare's), and the rhymed heroic couplets Milton derided. Often in the poem, Milton will have a sentence or clause ending mid line. The use of enjambment, unpredictable puns and repetitions of key words and carefully placed assonance and alliteration within single clauses creates powerful and often significant modulations in tone and meaning. The tension between the metrical rhythm and cadence of individual lines, at times complementing, at times running against the grain of ideas being expressed in the sentence running parallel, constantly calls on the reader to make conceptual adjustments and difficult, often ethical, interpretative decisions. These effects vary considerably within the poem, however, depending on the narrative context. As we will see in the commentary and analysis section in the next chapter, different characters and settings receive different stylistic treatments, like so many musical variations on a theme in a massive symphony. Satan's language, for example, is convoluted, rhetorically complex and often self-contradictory, while God's language tends towards balance, abstraction and logical clarity.

Finally, Milton deploys in the poem numerous poetic and literary devices, the most important of which are his frequent intertextual allusions and his elaborate epic similes. The allusive nature of *Paradise Lost* cannot be addressed in this *Guide*. Readers wishing to plumb the depths of Miltonic allusions are encouraged to consult, alongside this *Guide*, an annotated edition of the poem which gives the required information on some of the poem's more obscure allusions to classical mythology and literature, the Bible, or any number of other textual and scholarly sources and ideas. An annotated edition is especially needful, for example, to grasp the many proper names of ancient gods and geographical places such allusions often open up to. Although Milton evidently delighted to play metrically with proper names (the roll call of devils in Book I is one of the most stupendous and mesmerising of such catalogues), such allusions are never mere pedantry and decoration. As the study of Milton's allusions has consistently shown, each is carefully placed and often enriches the poem's deeper meanings in complex and unpredictable ways.

In this respect, Milton's epic similes have a similar function. In general, they are modelled in their digressive nature on the epic tradition of Homer and Virgil, but they depart from this tradition in a number of significant ways. The difference is largely in the direction and purpose of the comparison and the extent to which the Miltonic simile retains its shape *as* a simile. Homeric epic similes can fulfil a variety of functions, but they always remain anchored to the narrative plane of the poem. *Paradise Lost*, however, is a poem always running on two overlapping narrative levels: the one of the literal story narrating events prior to and leading up to the Fall, the other of the reader's necessarily fallen perception of that narrative. The principle which binds these two dimensions of the poem together is the idea of loss itself and of a material deficiency overcome by imaginative art. A primary function of Milton's epic similes is to anchor the literal level of the narrative into the reader's fallen metaphorical sensibilities, and as a consequence the similes which bind the two levels together are often proleptic, relying on the reader's prior knowledge of the story to complete the simile in their mind, thus heightening the pathos of the unfolding tragedy. For example, when in Book I the narrator compares the devils' military host gathering on a field in hell to 'locusts, warping on the eastern wind, / That o'er the realm of impious Pharaoh hung' (I. 341–2), the simile does not just diminish the devils to a plague of swarming insects, but raises innumerable proleptic 'fallen' connotations relating to the punishment due to all Pharaoh-like tyrants, to the exodus of the Israelites from bondage, and to the terror of God's wrath when sitting in judgement on those who disobey his will. It is also a deliberately confusing simile, since the image of a cloud of locusts 'warping' on the wind hardly suggests the military order and precision the devils' army pretends to but only a unity of destructive purpose of a mob being driven every which way by a greater force. Many of the similes in the poem work according to this proleptic model, but within this broad generalisation each simile is a world unto itself, introducing subtle but vital clues about the appropriate 'fallen' response to a given scene or speech. Because they always engage with the reader in demanding ways, many of Milton's epic similes may appear at first glance contradictory, imperfect or simply confusing. These effects, however, seem to be almost always carefully calculated and although some patterns emerge, especially with similes related to Satan and Eve, each simile requires close examination in its own right. When looking at any one of the epic similes in the poem, the reader needs first to identify the tenor and vehicle which would logically justify the simile to begin with, and then closely follow the logical trajectory of the simile *wherever* it leads. The reader has to be prepared to juggle in more complex cases multiple points of correspondence, similes nested within similes, and even similes which conjure a second or third silent simile that only emerges as a final, often destabilising implication (for a typical example see the analysis of Satan's whale simile in the commentary section in the next chapter).

Structural overview

Milton originally composed *Paradise Lost* in ten books, but revised the structure for the second edition of the poem published in 1674 (the last to be printed in Milton's lifetime) into twelve books, presumably to suit the classical model of Virgil's *Aeneid* (itself half of Homer's twenty-four book epic design). Superficially, the change from ten to twelve books was easily achieved by dividing the original Books VII and X into two books and then adding a few lines, for example in the beginning of Book VIII, to give the new structure greater balance. It is possible that the change from ten to twelve books, as many critics suppose, indicates a shift from a more dramatic structure of two five-act 'plays' to classical epic. Other meanings as well could be read into this change of structure. Alastair Fowler, for example, notes that the twelve-book structure of the 1674 edition creates two balanced six-book halves, each equally divided by an invocation to the muse into two and four books, thus bearing 'the diapason proportion 1:2, signifying harmony and control of passion'.[7] Whatever meaning one wishes to attach to the twelve-book structure, which is now the received form of the text most students and readers know, the four invocations to four very different muses at the opening of Books I, III, VII and IX clearly mark four distinct sections with differing dramatic and thematic characteristics. The resulting four parts are:

1. Books I–II – hell and Satan
2. Books III–VI – heaven, God and paradise before the Fall
3. Books VII–VIII – digression about the creation of the world
4. Books IX–XII – the Fall, punishment and prophetic visions of the future

The inspired narrator who governs our movement between these sections indicates the overall thematic and dramatic trajectory of each section. The impression is of a dizzying rising and falling movement which mirrors the central conceptual movement of loss at the heart of the poem's argument. We begin the first section by plunging down into the depths of hell. We then soar, in the second section, 'above all height', to heaven, only to descend more gently again into the prelapsarian bliss and equilibrium of Eden. Digressions at this stage take us back in time and up again into heaven, then down again in the third section into the creation of the world. The final, fourth, section then opens with the deepest plunge of all, as we witness the unfolding tragedy of the Fall and end very close to where we began, not in hell, but in the fallen world.

This basic four-section structure of the poem in its twelve-book form repeatedly requires that readers adjust to its shifting perspectives and accumulating hermeneutical effect. It also draws attention to different possible time schemes which shape the emerging narrative. Fowler has computed that the action of the poem, both before and after the Fall, amounts to a total of thirty-three days, where the end and beginning of each day, even in heaven before the creation of the world, is calculated by noting sunsets. The actual time scheme of the poem, however, is of esoteric interest; what matters is the sequence of events as they are presented to us. Had Milton opted to compose the narrative in a linear sequence, the poem would have been very different. The following table compares the linear, as opposed to the actual, sequence of events in the poem as we read it:

Linear narrative timeline of events	Actual order of events in the poem
God begets the Son and declares him Messiah	The devils awake in hell, regroup, build Pandaemonium and debate their next course of action (Books I–II)
Satan gathers a host of rebel angels and seduces them to revolt	Satan, having met his offspring Sin and Death, escapes hell across the gulf of Chaos and lands on the sun where he converses with the angel Uriel (Book II)
War breaks out in heaven between the rebel and obedient angels	The Father foresees the Fall of man and pronounces his future judgement, as the Son volunteers to redeem man from death (Book III)
The Messiah enters the battle, the rebels are routed and cast down to hell	Satan enters the Garden of Eden disguised as a cormorant, sees Adam and Eve and decides to cause their fall; he is then found by angels crouching by Eve's ear disguised as a toad whispering evil thoughts to her as she sleeps, and is expelled from the garden (Book IV)
The six days of creation in which God creates the world using the Son as his instrument, culminating with the creation of man on the sixth day	God sends Raphael to warn Adam and Eve and provide them with the necessary knowledge to resist temptation (Book V)

Linear narrative timeline of events	Actual order of events in the poem
The devils awake in hell, regroup, build Pandaemonium and debate their next course of action	Raphael discourses with Adam about the war in heaven which led to Satan's fall, explains about the creation of the world, warns about the limits of permissible knowledge and departs (Books V–VIII)
Satan, having met his offspring Sin and Death, escapes hell across the gulf of Chaos and lands on the sun where he converses with the angel Uriel	[beginning of Raphael's discourse:] God begets the Son and declares him Messiah (Book V)
The Father foresees the Fall of man and pronounces his future judgement, as the Son volunteers to redeem man from death	Satan gathers a host of rebel angels and seduces them to revolt (Book V)
Satan enters the Garden of Eden disguised as a cormorant, sees Adam and Eve and decides to cause their fall; he is then found by angels crouching by Eve's ear disguised as a toad whispering evil thoughts to her as she sleeps, and is expelled from the garden	War breaks out in heaven between the rebel and obedient angels (Books V–VI)
God sends Raphael to warn Adam and Eve and provide them with the necessary knowledge to resist temptation	The Messiah enters the battle, the rebels are routed and cast down to hell (Book VI)
Raphael discourses with Adam about the war in heaven which led to Satan's fall, explains about the creation of the world, warns about the limits of permissible knowledge and departs	The six days of creation in which God creates the world using the Son as his instrument, culminating with the creation of man on the sixth day (Books VII–VIII) [end of Raphael's discourse]
Satan re-enters the garden and tempts Eve disguised as a serpent; Eve next tempts Adam who decides to fall with her	Satan re-enters the garden and tempts Eve disguised as a serpent; Eve next tempts Adam who decides to fall with her (Book IX)

Linear narrative timeline of events	Actual order of events in the poem
The Son comes down into the garden to pass judgement on Adam and Eve; Sin and Death enter the world as Satan returns triumphant to hell; Adam and Eve lament and repent	The Son comes down into the garden to pass judgement on Adam and Eve; Sin and Death enter the world as Satan returns triumphant to hell; Adam and Eve lament and repent (Book X)
God sends Michael to set out before the fallen human couple a future vision of the world up to the Second Coming	God sends Michael to set out before the fallen human couple a future vision of the world up to the Second Coming (Book XI)
Adam and Eve are expelled from the garden	Adam and Eve are expelled from the garden (Book XII)

When comparing the linear sequence of events within the story to the order in which Milton arranges these events in the poem it becomes clear that it was never Milton's aim simply to tell a familiar biblical story with a few narrative embellishments; his aim was to retell a familiar biblical story in such a way as to fully engage his readers emotionally and intellectually in the main argument about disobedience and loss. The non-linear structure of the poem is meant to encourage an engaging interpretative process and to maximise its effect from the reader's point of view. Milton rearranges our narrative experience of the story's linear sequence so that our focus is always retained on the main action of the temptation leading up to the Fall in Book IX, while extensive digressions at crucial moments of the narrative fill us in on events before the creation which frame the human tragedy at the centre of the epic. The emphasis throughout is on carefully constructed points of view, almost like in a modern film where the same story is told from the different perspectives of individual characters remembering past events or experiencing present ones in real time. This narrative technique has the extraordinary effect of always filtering the immensity of the created universe, including even the ungraspable eternity and infinity of God, through the relative perspective of individual consciousness acting within the unfolding story, including, absurd as this might feel to some readers, the mind of God himself. This finally links back to different notions of time at work in the poem. Only before the Fall is it possible to talk of a linear progression of events unfolding in complete causal perspicuity according to the providential design of God. After the Fall, the providential design is still there, but human beings can no longer perceive its causality, except by inferring, deducting and intuiting elements of the providential plan by interpreting multiple and often contradictory signs within human history. The design of *Paradise Lost* ultimately lends itself to this heuristic experience, and ties in to the poem's central message about the responsibility and moral accountability that comes with recuperating rational free will after the Fall. As the narrator takes us on this remarkable journey through past biblical events and much else that takes place between the scriptural lines, it falls to us as readers, painfully made aware of our many human failings, to work out the final vision of providence and divine justice the poem offers to those willing and able to grasp it.

Notes

1. *CPW*, vii, p. 357.
2. Readers who wish to learn more about the manuscript and the knotty problems relating to its provenance should consult Gordon Campbell, Thomas N. Corns, John K. Hale and Fiona J. Tweedie, *Milton and the Manuscript of De Doctrina Christiana* (Oxford: Oxford University Press, 2007).
3. Milton coined this phrase in a very late prose treatise, *Of True Religion* (1673), in which he argued for wide religious nonconformity under the restored English Church. In the passage in question, Milton defends the various anti-Trinitarian sects not because he necessarily agrees with their theology, but because they reject the niceties of Trinitarian theology 'as Scholastic Notions, not to be found in Scripture, which by a general Protestant Maxim is plain and perspicuous abundantly to explain its own meaning in the properest words, belonging to so high a Matter and so necessary to be known; a mystery indeed in their Sophistic Subtilties, but in Scripture a plain Doctrin' (*CPW*, viii, pp. 424–5).
4. Readers can consult the Trinity Manuscript in facsimile. See *John Milton Poems: Reproduced in Facsimile from the Manuscript in Trinity College, Cambridge, with a Transcript,* ed. W. A. Wright (Menston, Ilkley: Scolar Press, 1970).
5. T. S. Eliot, 'A Note on the Verse of John Milton', reprinted in L. Martz (ed.), *Milton: A Collection of Critical Essays* (Englewood Cliffs, NJ: Prentice-Hall, 1966), pp. 12–18, at p. 18.
6. For more on this topic see the important article by John Creaser listed in the bibliography.
7. *Milton: Paradise Lost*, ed. Fowler, 2nd edn, p. 28.

Chapter 2

Text, Commentary and Analysis

The following commentary chapter centres on three sites of analysis in the poem and the different perspectives they offer to the reader within that whole: hell, heaven and paradise. As the outline of the poem's non-linear narrative structure in the previous chapter already indicates, each of these three sections represents a unique narrative and didactic dimension in the poem which is important for the overarching argument of the epic in different but complementary ways. The division into these three sections is not arbitrary. It is meant to offer readers a convenient way into the poem by teasing out the didactic structure already strongly implicit within the poem's monistic complex itself. The emerging settings of hell, heaven and paradise, filtered through competing voices and points of view, continually engage and implicate the reader in an ongoing process of re-education after the Fall. Throughout the commentary and analysis below, therefore, I will be drawing attention to the ways in which each of the three sections mirror and complicate each other. Each section reproduces substantial passages from the poem relevant to that section. The chosen passages are some of most famous and, in a few cases, controversial in the poem, and best highlight the major interpretative questions which arise in each case. Between them, the selected passages are meant to give readers a sense of the poem's manifold complexities, and of major 'flash points' in the text which have proved the most fertile for critical debate and analysis.

Hell, Satan, and the problem of evil

After the opening invocation to the 'Heav'nly Muse' (I. 6) and the exposition of the poem's 'great argument', Milton hurls his readers alongside a falling Satan, 'With hideous ruin and combustion down / To bottomless perdition' (I. 46–7). With words of prophecy and inspiration still ringing in our ears, the first image that opens up before us in the poem is that of Satan, stunned from his fall, weltering on a burning lake. Milton opens his epic with the horrors of hell and the remarkable, heroic grandeur of its 'new possessor' (I. 252). Milton's strategy in the two opening books of the epic is calculated to confront his readers with an immediate ethical choice: whether or not to identify with Satan, 'the infernal serpent', who is, as the narrator declares at the outset, unequivocally responsible for seducing man 'to that foul revolt' (I. 33) which lost humanity its place in paradise. Given that the narrator clearly informs us that Satan is the evil agent responsible for man's ruin it is perhaps surprising that initial reactions to Milton's great anti-hero have often been divided. Just as there are always readers happy to accept the narrator's framing argument at face value, there have been an equal number of readers – most famously perhaps the Romantic poets Blake and Shelley, and closer to our time the author Philip Pullman – who believe that Satan is clearly the sympathetic figure of the epic and that Milton was therefore, to quote Blake's famous words, of the 'Devil's party without knowing it', or worse, knowingly of the devil's party.[1]

How we interpret the *function* of Satan in the poem to a large extent reflects on how we understand the poem's most fundamental didactic aims. In the twentieth century this debate found its most polarised and most famous expression in the post-war criticism of C. S. Lewis and William Empson, respectively. Lewis, a devout Christian, denounced all readers who sympathise with Satan as misguided atheists who in their satanic attacks on Milton's God masked their hatred of God himself. Empson, a self-professed atheist, essentially confirmed Lewis's thesis by turning it upside down and arguing that Milton's Satan heroically and justly rebels against the tyranny of an evil Christian God, whom Milton succeeds in making only marginally less repellent in the poem than he is in actual religious belief. Lewis and Empson galvanised the debate and collected adherents on both sides, until the debate was provisionally settled, or at the very least directed elsewhere, by American critic and reader-response theorist Stanley E. Fish.

In *Surprised by Sin: The Reader in* Paradise Lost (1967), Fish proposed the powerful thesis that Lewis and Empson were in a sense both right and wrong, since they were both victims of a deliberate literary strategy which Milton deploys in the poem aimed at entrapping the unsuspecting reader in their own sense of fallen sinfulness (not to say righteousness). According to Fish, Milton wants his readers not just to hear a sermon about the loss of paradise, but actually to experience the shame and enormity of the tragedy on a personal level, and he achieves this chiefly by encouraging the reader to sympathise with Satan and then putting into play counter-narratives and voices which force the 'harassed' reader to confront this sinful sense of sympathy and shamefully regret it. According to Fish's paradigm, therefore, what Milton could never anticipate is that some readers, while entirely convinced of the sympathetic Satan, like Empson and Pullman simply refuse to play along when they are called upon by the poem to feel shame for such allegedly misplaced emotions.

Whatever reader response Milton's Satan elicits, it is unquestionable that he is the most vividly realised character of the epic. Satan's dazzling rhetorical displays and anguished and very relatable efforts to confront the inexorability of his damnation draw us in as auditors. Much of the tragic sympathy Milton's Satan stirs in readers results from the tension in the poem between Satan's relatable physicality and tormented, almost Shakespearean interiority on the one hand, and his conceptual-mythological role as the arch devil and a figure of primordial evil on the other. Whatever the theology of the poem might lead us to think about Satan as the *cause* of all evil in God's good creation, we are nevertheless struck by his overriding *personality*, and there are moments in the poem where his personality certainly overshadows and flattens the abstractions on which divine justice depends. This tension can also work to arouse sympathy towards Satan in another way. Part of Satan's tragedy as Milton presents it is that his very real physical presence and his compelling rhetorical energy founder in a hell which is both an intangible state of mind and a paradoxical non-place of eternal exclusion. Milton's hell is a place of negation and hollowness, where flames give no light and tempests have no sound, imagined as the negative space created by God, ominously, 'by curse' (II. 622). In such a scheme, every expression of Satan's human physicality and emotional complexity strikes in many readers a moving chord of loss precisely because of the epic settings of hell and paradise against which the pathos of these expressions is measured. However, as the argument between Lewis and Empson mentioned above already indicates, such reactions tend to be filtered through a necessarily wide spectrum of prejudices. Depending on a reader's perspective, Satan's tragedy can equally arouse feelings of sympathy for his impossible plight, as well as feelings of guarded relief for those readers who accept God's justice (whether as a precondition of the text or as a matter of personal faith). The poem's theological bias in this respect is unequivocal. In Book III, Milton's God declares that unlike Satan and the rebel angels who are 'Self-tempted, self-depraved' and have no hope of redemption, man 'falls deceived' and 'therefore shall find grace'

(III. 130–1). Such words do more than set up a theological framework for negotiating the poem's main argument about divine justice – they can also be read as addressed to the reader who is anxiously seeking to rationalise his potentially sinful identification with humanity's arch-enemy.

Key passages

1. Book I. 81–330

It is Satan then, not God or Adam, who first commands our attention in the poem and the power and dignity which his words exude can be so overwhelming that many readers are immediately won to his side and wish to remain there even when confronted by clear indications in the poem that to do so is damnable. The following passage from the opening book slowly builds the image of the once heroic Satan, his 'excess / Of glory obscured' (I. 593–4), wounded in his sense of 'injured merit' (98), trying to recover his wits and pride after his fall and to process the enormity of the loss inflicted on him and his fallen comrades. His opening dialogue with Beelzebub, his second in command lying next to him on the lake of fire, astounds with its tone of defiance and apparent courage in the face of devastating and logically inevitable defeat. That Satan should continue to contemplate ways to defeat and frustrate an omnipotent, omniscient God might be seen by many, quite rightly, as hopelessly futile, but there is also something inspiring, not to say genuinely poetic, about the desperate defiance of a rebel who declares that it is 'Better to reign in Hell, than serve in Heav'n' (I. 263). One need only think of Shelley's Prometheus or Albert Camus's Sisyphus to appreciate just how inspiring such impossible defiance was for Romantic or existential writers in later periods. Milton, however, writes into the opening Satanic speeches and dialogues nuanced words and images which belay Satan's heroic bravado and point to the ethical and spiritual vacuity which besets his personality. The entire opening sequence of the epic, reproduced in part below, is conducted under the erasure of Satan's angelic identity. His given angelic name of Lucifer has now been blotted out forever and replaced in heaven with the biblical Hebrew for adversary, 'Satan'. Satan has lost more than just a name, however. In rebelling against the divine will he has forfeited the glory that comes from angelic proximity with God, leaving him an empty shell of self-loving idolatry, 'Vaunting aloud, but racked with deep despair' (I. 126). Deep despair is the key to this passage and the setting of hell altogether, because it creeps not just on Satan but on the reader as well. As we shall see in the

commentary section below, its deepness is felt in Satan's constant shifty
use of double negatives and false logic in his reasoning, in the beautiful but dark Leviathan and moon similes which give Satan a ponderous
aura of hidden danger but also of deception and illusion, and in the
tone and imagery of the poetry throughout, which gives the impression
of futile movement and inexorability as it weighs in our view Satan's
former glory with his present shame.

> To whom th' Arch-Enemy,
> And thence in Heav'n called Satan, with bold words
> Breaking the horrid silence thus began.
>   If thou beest he; but O how fall'n! how changed
> From him, who in the happy realms of light   [85]
> Clothed with transcendent brightness didst outshine
> Myriads though bright: if he whom mutual league,
> United thoughts and counsels, equal hope
> And hazard in the glorious enterprise,
> Joined with me once, now misery hath joined   [90]
> In equal ruin: into what pit thou seest
> From what heighth fall'n, so much the stronger proved
> He with his thunder: and till then who knew
> The force of those dire arms? yet not for those,
> Nor what the potent Victor in his rage   [95]
> Can else inflict, do I repent or change,
> Though changed in outward lustre, that fixed mind
> And high disdain, from sense of injured merit,
> That with the mightiest raised me to contend,
> And to the fierce contention brought along   [100]
> Innumerable force of Spirits armed
> That durst dislike his reign, and me preferring,
> His utmost power with adverse power opposed
> In dubious battle on the plains of Heav'n,
> And shook his throne. What though the field be lost?   [105]
> All is not lost; the unconquerable will,
> And study of revenge, immortal hate,
> And courage never to submit or yield:
> And what is else not to be overcome?
> That glory never shall his wrath or might   [110]
> Extort from me. To bow and sue for grace
> With suppliant knee, and deify his power
> Who from the terror of this arm so late
> Doubted his empire, that were low indeed,
> That were an ignominy and shame beneath   [115]
> This downfall; since by Fate the strength of gods

And this empyreal substance cannot fail,
Since through experience of this great event
In arms not worse, in foresight much advanced,
We may with more successful hope resolve   [120]
To wage by force or guile eternal war
Irreconcilable, to our grand Foe,
Who now triúmphs, and in th' excess of joy
Sole reigning holds the tyranny of Heav'n.
        So spake th' apostate angel, though in pain,   [125]
Vaunting aloud, but racked with deep despair:
And him thus answered soon his bold compeer.
        O Prince, O chief of many thronèd Powers
That led th' embattled Seraphim to war
Under thy conduct, and in dreadful deeds   [130]
Fearless, endangered Heav'n's perpetual King;
And put to proof his high supremacy,
Whether upheld by strength, or Chance, or Fate;
Too well I see and rue the dire event,
That with sad overthrow and foul defeat   [135]
Hath lost us Heav'n, and all this mighty host
In horrible destruction laid thus low,
As far as gods and Heav'nly essences
Can perish: for the mind and spirit remains
Invincible, and vigour soon returns,   [140]
Though all our glory extinct, and happy state
Here swallowed up in endless misery.
But what if he our Conqueror, (whom I now
Of force believe Almighty, since no less
Than such could have o'erpow'red such force as ours)   [145]
Have left us this our spirit and strength entire
Strongly to suffer and support our pains,
That we may so suffice his vengeful ire,
Or do him mightier service as his thralls
By right of war, whate'er his business be,   [150]
Here in the heart of Hell to work in fire,
Or do his errands in the gloomy deep;
What can it then avail though yet we feel
Strength undiminished, or eternal being
To undergo eternal punishment?   [155]
Whereto with speedy words th' Arch-Fiend replied.
        Fall'n Cherub, to be weak is miserable
Doing or suffering: but of this be sure,
To do aught good never will be our task,
But ever to do ill our sole delight,   [160]

As being the contrary to his high will
Whom we resist. If then his Providence
Out of our evil seek to bring forth good,
Our labour must be to pervert that end,
And out of good still to find means of evil,   [165]
Which oft-times may succeed, so as perhaps
Shall grieve him, if I fail not, and disturb
His inmost counsels from their destined aim.
But see the angry Victor hath recalled
His ministers of vengeance and pursuit   [170]
Back to the gates of Heav'n: the sulphurous hail
Shot after us in storm, o'erblown hath laid
The fiery surge, that from the precipice
Of Heav'n received us falling, and the thunder
Winged with red lightning and impetuous rage,   [175]
Perhaps has spent his shafts, and ceases now
To bellow though the vast and boundless deep.
Let us not slip th' occasion, whether scorn,
Or satiate fury yield it from our Foe.
Seest thou yon dreary plain, forlorn and wild,   [180]
The seat of desolation, void of light,
Save what the glimmering of these livid flames
Casts pale and dreadful? Thither let us tend
From off the tossing of these fiery waves,
There rest, if any rest can harbour there,   [185]
And reassembling our afflicted powers,
Consult how we may henceforth most offend
Our Enemy, our own loss how repair,
How overcome this dire calamity,
What reinforcement we may gain from hope,   [190]
If not what resolution from despair.
      Thus Satan talking to his nearest mate
With head uplift above the wave, and eyes
That sparkling blazed; his other parts besides
Prone on the flood, extended long and large   [195]
Lay floating many a rood, in bulk as huge
As whom the fables name of monstrous size,
Titanian, or Earth-born, that warred on Jove,
Briareos or Typhon, whom the den
By ancient Tarsus held, or that sea-beast   [200]
Leviathan, which God of all his works
Created hugest that swim th' Océan stream:
Him haply slumb'ring on the Norway foam
The pilot of some small night-foundered skiff,

Deeming some island, oft, as seamen tell,   [205]
With fixèd anchor in his scaly rind
Moors by his side under the lee, while night
Invests the sea, and wishèd morn delays:
So stretched out huge in length the Arch-Fiend lay
Chained on the burning lake, nor ever thence   [210]
Had ris'n or heaved his head, but that the will
And high permission of all-ruling Heaven
Left him at large to his own dark designs,
That with reiterated crimes he might
Heap on himself damnation, while he sought   [215]
Evil to others, and enraged might see
How all his malice served but to bring forth
Infinite goodness, grace and mercy shown
On man by him seduced, but on himself
Treble confusion, wrath and vengeance poured.   [220]
Forthwith upright he rears from off the pool
His mighty stature; on each hand the flames
Driv'n backward slope their pointing spires, and rolled
In billows, leave i' th' midst a horrid vale.
      Then with expanded wings he steers his flight   [225]
Aloft, incumbent on the dusky air
That felt unusual weight, till on dry land
He lights, if it were land that ever burned
With solid, as the lake with liquid fire,
And such appeared in hue; as when the force   [230]
Of subterranean wind transports a hill
Torn from Pelorus, or the shattered side
Of thund'ring Etna, whose combustible
And fuelled entrails thence conceiving fire,
Sublimed with mineral fury, aid the winds,   [235]
And leave a singèd bottom all involved
With stench and smoke: such resting found the sole
Of unblest feet. Him followed his next mate,
Both glorying to have 'scaped the Stygian flood
As gods, and by their own recovered strength,   [240]
Not by the sufferance of supernal power.
      Is this the region, this the soil, the clime,
Said then the lost Archangel, this the seat
That we must change for Heav'n, this mournful gloom
For that celestial light? Be it so, since he   [245]
Who now is sov'reign can dispose and bid
What shall be right: farthest from him is best
Whom reason hath equalled, force hath made supreme

Above his equals. Farewell happy fields
Where joy forever dwells: hail horrors, hail   [250]
Infernal world, and thou profoundest Hell
Receive thy new possessor: one who brings
A mind not to be changed by place or time.
The mind is its own place, and in itself
Can make a Heav'n of Hell, a Hell of Heav'n.   [255]
What matter where, if I be still the same,
And what I should be, all but less than he
Whom thunder hath made greater? Here at least
We shall be free; th' Almighty hath not built
Here for his envy, will not drive us hence: [260]
Here we may reign secure, and in my choice
To reign is worth ambition though in Hell:
Better to reign in Hell, than serve in Heav'n.
But wherefore let we then our faithful friends,
Th' associates and copartners of our loss   [265]
Lie thus astonished on th' oblivious pool,
And call them not to share with us their part
In this unhappy mansion; or once more
With rallied arms to try what may be yet
Regained in Heav'n, or what more lost in Hell?   [270]
    So Satan spake, and him Beëlzebub
Thus answered. Leader of those armies bright,
Which but th' Omnipotent none could have foiled,
If once they hear that voice, their liveliest pledge
Of hope in fears and dangers, heard so oft   [275]
In worst extremes, and on the perilous edge
Of battle when it raged, in all assaults
Their surest signal, they will soon resume
New courage and revive, though now they lie
Grovelling and prostrate on yon lake of fire,   [280]
As we erewhile, astounded and amazed,
No wonder, fall'n such a pernicious heighth.
    He scarce had ceased when the superior fiend
Was moving toward the shore; his ponderous shield
Ethereal temper, massy, large and round,   [285]
Behind him cast; the broad circumference
Hung on his shoulders like the moon, whose orb
Through optic glass the Tuscan artist views
At evening from the top of Fesole,
Or in Valdarno, to descry new lands,   [290]
Rivers or mountains in her spotty globe.
His spear, to equal which the tallest pine

Hewn on Norwegian hills, to be the mast
Of some great ammiral, were but a wand,
He walked with to support uneasy steps   [295]
Over the burning marl, not like those steps
On Heav'n's azure; and the torrid clime
Smote on him sore besides, vaulted with fire;
Nathless he so endured, till on the beach
Of that inflamèd sea, he stood and called   [300]
His legions, angel forms, who lay entranced
Thick as autumnal leaves that strow the brooks
In Vallombrosa, where th' Etrurian shades
High overarched embow'r; or scattered sedge
Afloat, when with fierce winds Orion armed   [305]
Hath vexed the Red Sea coast, whose waves o'erthrew
Busiris and his Memphian chivalry,
While with perfidious hatred they pursued
The sojourners of Goshen, who beheld
From the safe shore their floating carcasses   [310]
And broken chariot wheels. So thick bestrown
Abject and lost lay these, covering the flood,
Under amazement of their hideous change.
He called so loud, that all the hollow deep
Of Hell resounded. Princes, Potentates,   [315]
Warriors, the flow'r of Heav'n, once yours, now lost,
If such astonishment as this can seize
Eternal Spirits: or have ye chos'n this place
After the toil of battle to repose
Your wearied virtue, for the ease you find   [320]
To slumber here, as in the vales of Heav'n?
Or in this abject posture have ye sworn
To adore the Conqueror? who now beholds
Cherub and Seraph rolling in the flood
With scattered arms and ensigns, till anon   [325]
His swift pursuers from Heav'n gates discern
Th' advantage, and descending tread us down
Thus drooping, or with linkèd thunderbolts
Transfix us to the bottom of this gulf.
Awake, arise, or be for ever fall'n.   [330]

2. *Book II. 643–889*

Milton's animist monism (see Chapter 1) is not just a conceptual idea
which governs the philosophical and theological framework of *Paradise
Lost*, but also a major principle of its poetics. Milton's imagined

universe, encompassing hell, heaven, and paradise, is bound within a single narrative vision relying heavily on tactile and material imagery to convey the idea of one continuous matter. From the burning 'marl' of hell's pit, through the 'liquid pearl' of the stairs leading up to heaven's gate, to the 'vegetable gold' of the Garden of Eden, the poem gives the impression of a great baroque work of art crafted from innumerable materials which become more fantastic (and presumably more attenuated) the farther the vision extends from a recognisable fallen earth. This also impacts on the status of metaphor in the poem because if in the imagined universe of the poem body (vehicle) and spirit (tenor) are said to be relative and co-substantial rather than distinct, then metaphors which substitute between their vehicles and tenors, rather than simply comparing between them in a simile, cannot function. By insisting on these monistic imperatives, Milton promotes in the poem the conceit that the reader is confronted throughout with literal truth as opposed to mere literary representation. Such material concreteness, however, is mostly confined to the prelapsarian dimension of the poem and is undermined significantly by the incongruous presence of allegory, especially in the personification of Sin and Death.

Satan first encounters these grotesque figures guarding the gate of hell as he attempts to escape upward into the world (with God's silent permission) in the hope of marring somehow God's recent creation. A number of theories have been proposed to explain the presence of such blatantly Spenserian allegorical figures in a poem so plainly counter-allegorical in its scheme. It is certainly significant that allegory is confined to hell. Milton follows James 1: 15 ('Then when lust has conceived, it bringeth forth sin: and sin, when it is finished, bringeth forth death') in creatively mythologising the central Pauline concepts of sin and death as demonic beings conceived from an incestuous union. Milton portrays Sin as a perversely maternal 'snaky sorceress' (II. 724) which has much of Spenser's Error in her, and Death as a shadowy, shapeless abomination of hate and terror, wielding a deadly dart and already wearing a royal crown alluding to his future dominion of the world. In the following passage, the narrator describes these two figures for the first time in the poem, as well as the ensuing 'family reunion' between Satan and his two diabolic offspring. This reunion, stirring in Satan what can only be deeply repressed memories, forces him to recognise the dreadful consequences of his rebellion. We learn that Sin (whose name in the passage below forms a disturbing pun on 'sign') was born, Athena-like, from Satan's head at the instant of his rebellion against God, while Death was conceived from the incestuous union of

Satan with his 'daughter'. Normally, we expect allegory to act as an extended metaphor which embeds hidden meanings within the text that only a privileged reader with the required allegorical key (usually a set of abstract philosophical and/or theological ideas) can unlock. Allegory by nature is unstable since it lends itself to a near endless proliferation of meaning beyond the text, but in *Paradise Lost* Sin and Death are finally dysfunctional allegories because they point to nothing but their own destabilising presence in the poem. Their slippery indeterminacy in the passage below is made all the more terrifying, therefore, when set against the material solidity of the impenetrable gate they guard. It is a gate which separates their nether world of eviscerated flesh and truth from God's created world of absolute literal truth. After the Fall, this gate will be permanently breached as Sin and Death spill into the fallen world, darkening divine truth with their corrupting allegorical presence even as they themselves assume an all too real and substantial form in human life as existential presences. This future corruption is anticipated throughout this sequence in the travesty of God's monarchy in heaven. Satan's begetting of Sin, who hopes to sit one day at his right hand, is a dark mockery of the Father's begetting of the Son narrated later in Book V, who also sits on the right hand of the Father. The Son, moreover, is contrasted here with Satan's 'son', Death, over whom the Son will have final victory at the end of days, but not it seems for a very long time, and not while art and poetry have a role to play in the world.

>   . . . at last appear
> Hell bounds high reaching to the horrid roof,
> And thrice threefold the gates; three folds were brass,   [645]
> Three iron, three of adamantine rock,
> Impenetrable, impaled with circling fire,
> Yet unconsumed. Before the gates there sat
> On either side a formidable shape;
> The one seemed woman to the waist, and fair,   [650]
> But ended foul in many a scaly fold
> Voluminous and vast, a serpent armed
> With mortal sting: about her middle round
> A cry of Hell-hounds never ceasing barked
> With wide Cerberean mouths full loud, and rung   [655]
> A hideous peal: yet, when they list, would creep,
> If aught disturbed their noise, into her womb,
> And kennel there, yet there still barked and howled
> Within unseen. Far less abhorred than these
> Vexed Scylla bathing in the sea that parts   [660]

Calabria from the hoarse Trinacrian shore:
Nor uglier follow the night-hag, when called
In secret, riding through the air she comes
Lured with the smell of infant blood, to dance
With Lapland witches, while the labouring moon   [665]
Eclipses at their charms. The other shape,
If shape it might be called that shape had none
Distinguishable in member, joint, or limb,
Or substance might be called that shadow seemed,
For each seemed either; black it stood as Night,   [670]
Fierce as ten Furies, terrible as Hell,
And shook a dreadful dart; what seemed his head
The likeness of a kingly crown had on.
Satan was now at hand, and from his seat
The monster moving onward came as fast   [675]
With horrid strides, Hell trembled as he strode.
Th' undaunted Fiend what this might be admired,
Admired, not feared; God and his Son except,
Created thing naught valued he nor shunned;
And with disdainful look thus first began.   [680]
        Whence and what art thou, execrable shape,
That dar'st though grim and terrible, advance
Thy miscreated front athwart my way
To yonder gates? Through them I mean to pass,
That be assured, without leave asked of thee: [685]
Retire, or taste thy folly, and learn by proof,
Hell-born, not to contend with Spirits of Heav'n.
        To whom the goblin full of wrath replied,
Art thou that traitor angel, art thou he,
Who first broke peace in Heav'n and faith, till then   [690]
Unbroken, and in proud rebellious arms
Drew after him the third part of Heav'n's sons
Conjúred against the Highest, for which both thou
And they outcást from God, are here condemned
To waste eternal days in woe and pain?   [695]
And reckon'st thou thyself with Spirits of Heav'n,
Hell-doomed, and breath'st defiance here and scorn,
Where I reign king, and to enrage thee more,
Thy king and lord? Back to thy punishment,
False fugitive, and to thy speed add wings,   [700]
Lest with a whip of scorpions I pursue
Thy ling'ring, or with one stroke of this dart
Strange horror seize thee, and pangs unfelt before.
        So spake the grisly terror, and in shape,

So speaking and so threat'ning, grew tenfold   [705]
More dreadful and deform: on th' other side
Incensed with indignation Satan stood
Unterrified, and like a comet burned,
That fires the length of Ophiucus huge
In th' Arctic sky, and from his horrid hair   [710]
Shakes pestilence and war. Each at the head
Levelled his deadly aim; their fatal hands
No second stroke intend, and such a frown
Each cast at th' other, as when two black clouds
With heav'n's artillery fraught, come rattling on   [715]
Over the Caspian, then stand front to front
Hov'ring a space, till winds the signal blow
To join their dark encounter in mid air:
So frowned the mighty combatants, that Hell
Grew darker at their frown, so matched they stood;   [720]
For never but once more was either like
To meet so great a foe: and now great deeds
Had been achieved, whereof all Hell had rung,
Had not the snaky sorceress that sat
Fast by Hell gate, and kept the fatal key,   [725]
Ris'n, and with hideous outcry rushed between.
      O father, what intends thy hand, she cried,
Against thy only son? What fury O son,
Possesses thee to bend that mortal dart
Against thy father's head? and know'st for whom;   [730]
For him who sits above and laughs the while
At thee ordained his drudge, to execute
Whate'er his wrath, which he calls justice, bids,
His wrath which one day will destroy ye both.
      She spake, and at her words the Hellish pest   [735]
Forbore, then these to her Satan returned:
      So strange thy outcry, and thy words so strange
Thou interposest, that my sudden hand
Prevented spares to tell thee yet by deeds
What it intends; till first I know of thee,   [740]
What thing thou art, thus double-formed, and why
In this infernal vale first met thou call'st
Me father, and that phantasm call'st my son?
I know thee not, nor ever saw till now
Sight more detestable than him and thee.   [745]
      T' whom thus the portress of Hell gate replied;
Hast thou forgot me then, and do I seem
Now in thine eye so foul, once deemed so fair

In Heav'n, when at th' assembly, and in sight
Of all the Seraphim with thee combined   [750]
In bold conspiracy against Heav'n's King,
All on a sudden miserable pain
Surprised thee, dim thine eyes, and dizzy swum
In darkness, while thy head flames thick and fast
Threw forth, till on the left side op'ning wide,   [755]
Likest to thee in shape and count'nance bright,
Then shining Heav'nly fair, a goddess armed
Out of thy head I sprung: amazement seized
All th' host of Heav'n; back they recoiled afraid
At first, and called me *Sin,* and for a Sign   [760]
Portentous held me; but familiar grown,
I pleased, and with attractive graces won
The most averse, thee chiefly, who full oft
Thyself in me thy perfect image viewing
Becam'st enamoured, and such joy thou took'st   [765]
With me in secret, that my womb conceived
A growing burden. Meanwhile war arose,
And fields were fought in Heav'n; wherein remained
(For what could else) to our Almighty Foe
Clear victory, to our part loss and rout   [770]
Through all the Empyrean: down they fell
Driv'n headlong from the pitch of Heaven, down
Into this deep, and in the general fall
I also; at which time this powerful key
Into my hand was giv'n, with charge to keep   [775]
These gates for ever shut, which none can pass
Without my op'ning. Pensive here I sat
Alone, but long I sat not, till my womb
Pregnant by thee, and now excessive grown
Prodigious motion felt and rueful throes.   [780]
At last this odious offspring whom thou seest
Thine own begotten, breaking violent way
Tore through my entrails, that with fear and pain
Distorted, all my nether shape thus grew
Transformed: but he my inbred enemy   [785]
Forth issued, brandishing his fatal dart
Made to destroy: I fled, and cried out *Death*;
Hell trembled at the hideous name, and sighed
Through all her caves, and back resounded *Death*.
I fled, but he pursued (though more, it seems,   [790]
Inflamed with lust than rage) and swifter far,
Me overtook his mother all dismayed,

And in embraces forcible and foul
Engend'ring with me, of that rape begot
These yelling monsters that with ceaseless cry   [795]
Surround me, as thou saw'st, hourly conceived
And hourly born, with sorrow infinite
To me, for when they list into the womb
That bred them they return, and howl and gnaw
My bowels, their repast; then bursting forth   [800]
Afresh with conscious terrors vex me round,
That rest or intermission none I find.
Before mine eyes in opposition sits
Grim Death my son and foe, who sets them on,
And me his parent would full soon devour   [805]
For want of other prey, but that he knows
His end with mine involved; and knows that I
Should prove a bitter morsel, and his bane,
Whenever that shall be; so Fate pronounced.
But thou O father, I forewarn thee, shun   [810]
His deadly arrow; neither vainly hope
To be invulnerable in those bright arms,
Though tempered Heav'nly, for that mortal dint,
Save he who reigns above, none can resist.
    She finished, and the subtle Fiend his lore   [815]
Soon learned, now milder, and thus answered smooth.
Dear daughter, since thou claim'st me for thy sire,
And my fair son here show'st me, the dear pledge
Of dalliance had with thee in Heav'n, and joys
Then sweet, now sad to mention, through dire change   [820]
Befall'n us unforeseen, unthought of, know
I come no enemy, but to set free
From out this dark and dismal house of pain,
Both him and thee, and all the Heav'nly host
Of Spirits that in our just pretences armed   [825]
Fell with us from on high: from them I go
This uncouth errand sole, and one for all
Myself expose, with lonely steps to tread
Th' unfounded deep, and through the void immense
To search with wand'ring quest a place foretold   [830]
Should be, and, by concurring signs, ere now
Created vast and round, a place of bliss
In the purlieus of Heav'n, and therein placed
A race of upstart creatures, to supply
Perhaps our vacant room, though more removed,   [835]
Least Heav'n surcharged with potent multitude

Might hap to move new broils: be this or aught
Than this more secret now designed, I haste
To know, and this once known, will soon return,
And bring ye to the place where thou and Death   [840]
Shall dwell at ease, and up and down unseen
Wing silently the buxom air, embalmed
With odours; there ye shall be fed and filled
Immeasurably, all things shall be your prey.
He ceased, for both seemed highly pleased, and Death   [845]
Grinned horrible a ghastly smile, to hear
His famine should be filled, and blessed his maw
Destined to that good hour: no less rejoiced
His mother bad, and thus bespake her sire.
    The key of this infernal pit by due,   [850]
And by command of Heav'n's all-powerful King
I keep, by him forbidden to unlock
These adamantine gates: against all force
Death ready stands to interpose his dart,
Fearless to be o'ermatched by living might.   [855]
But what owe I to his commands above
Who hates me, and hath hither thrust me down
Into this gloom of Tartarus profound,
To sit in hateful office here confined,
Inhabitant of Heav'n, and Heav'nly-born,   [860]
Here in perpetual agony and pain,
With terrors and with clamors compassed round
Of mine own brood, that on my bowels feed:
Thou art my father, thou my author, thou
My being gav'st me; whom should I obey   [865]
But thee, whom follow? thou wilt bring me soon
To that new world of light and bliss, among
The gods who live at ease, where I shall reign
At thy right hand voluptuous, as beseems
Thy daughter and thy darling, without end.   [870]
    Thus saying, from her side the fatal key,
Sad instrument of all our woe, she took;
And towards the gate rolling her bestial train,
Forthwith the huge portcullis high up drew,
Which but herself not all the Stygian powers   [875]
Could once have moved; then in the key-hole turns
Th' intricate wards, and every bolt and bar
Of massy iron or solid rock with ease
Unfastens: on a sudden open fly
With impetuous recoil and jarring sound   [880]

Th' infernal doors, and on their hinges grate
Harsh thunder, that the lowest bottom shook
Of Erebus. She opened, but to shut
Excelled her power; the gates wide open stood,
That with extended wings a bannered host   [885]
Under spread ensigns marching might pass through
With horse and chariots ranked in loose array;
So wide they stood, and like a furnace mouth
Cast forth redounding smoke and ruddy flame.

3. Book IV. 1–130

After Satan escapes from hell, he begins his solitary journey across the
abyss of Chaos, upwards towards the gate of heaven, where disguised
as an angel he coaxes information about God's creation from the archangel Uriel, guardian of the sun. After receiving directions, he finally
descends into the created world and paradise. There he alights on the
top of Mount Niphates from which he surveys the literally new world
spread beneath him. Alone with his thoughts, Satan has no audience to
impress, no army of fallen angels to rouse with stirring speeches. Like
a Shakespearean soliloquising villain, Satan now moves beyond the
shimmering haze of his rhetoric in the earlier books into close intimacy
with the reader, and we see him for what he is: tormented, wracked by
guilt and despair, and all too 'human'. There is biographical evidence
to suggest that Milton wrote part of Satan's Mount Niphates soliloquy
at an earlier stage when he was still thinking of *Paradise Lost* as a dramatic poem.[2] In the soliloquy Satan reflects on his state of damnation
and 'at length confirms himself in evil' (Milton's 'Argument' to Book
IV). It is one of the most poignant and moving passages in the poem
and it is the most effective in arousing sympathy for a now vulnerable
Satan, as it dramatises his complex struggle with fleeting, albeit purely
theoretical, thoughts of repentance – theoretical both because the
road of repentance is closed to him, and because his pride is too great
anyway. The sense of tragedy attached to the soliloquy is filtered in
this passage not just through Shakespearean allusion and tone but also
through a theological language saturated with the Calvinist rhetoric of
reprobation. It suits Milton's anti-Calvinist Arminian thinking that in
abusing his free will by rebelling against his creator Satan has forfeited
his freedom and is now bound to the Calvinist terror of irrevocable
damnation (see especially lines 66–70). The light of the sun (always a
pun in the poem on 'Son') with its lesser created glory instantly conjures
for Satan painful memories of the heavenly light from which he is now

excluded. The light imagery finally reflects on Satan's lack of inner illumination. Recoiling upon himself like a 'devilish engine' (IV. 17), Satan looks inwards and discovers that hell is first and foremost a darkness of the mind. 'Engine' is a striking and suggestive word in this context. It suggests a malfunctioning mechanical device, or an abortive devilish plot, and it alludes finally to the empty mechanistic shell Satan's interiority has been reduced to following his ejection from heaven. The didactic implications of such a reading are anticipated and reinforced by the opening lines of the book, where the narrator quotes the verses of Revelations 8: 13, warning humanity of the destructive falling star Wormwood. The narrator frames in this way Satan's soliloquies within the context of biblical prophecy, pointing up the potential horror and danger for all of fallen humanity in this crucial moment of Satan's transformation from heroic and tragic persona into a theological representation of pure evil.

O for that warning voice, which he who saw
Th' Apocalypse, heard cry in Heav'n aloud,
Then when the Dragon, put to second rout,
Came furious down to be revenged on men,
Woe to the inhabitants on earth! that now,   [5]
While time was, our first parents had been warned
The coming of their secret foe, and 'scaped
Haply so 'scaped his mortal snare; for now
Satan, now first inflamed with rage, came down,
The Tempter ere th' Accuser of mankind,   [10]
To wreck on innocent frail man his loss
Of that first battle, and his flight to Hell:
Yet not rejoicing in his speed, though bold,
Far off and fearless, nor with cause to boast,
Begins his dire attempt, which nigh the birth   [15]
Now rolling, boils in his tumultuous breast,
And like a devilish engine back recoils
Upon himself; horror and doubt distract
His troubled thoughts, and from the bottom stir
The Hell within him, for within him Hell   [20]
He brings, and round about him, nor from Hell
One step no more than from himself can fly
By change of place: now conscience wakes despair
That slumbered, wakes the bitter memory
Of what he was, what is, and what must be   [25]
Worse; of worse deeds worse sufferings must ensue.
Sometimes towards Eden which now in his view

Lay pleasant, his grieved look he fixes sad,
Sometimes towards heav'n and the full-blazing sun,
Which now sat high in his meridian tower: [30]
Then much revolving, thus in sighs began.
    O thou that with surpassing glory crowned,
Look'st from thy sole dominion like the God
Of this new world; at whose sight all the stars
Hide their diminished heads; to thee I call,   [35]
But with no friendly voice, and add thy name
O sun, to tell thee how I hate thy beams
That bring to my remembrance from what state
I fell, how glorious once above thy sphere;
Till pride and worse ambition threw me down   [40]
Warring in Heav'n against Heav'n's matchless King:
Ah wherefore! he deserved no such return
From me, whom he created what I was
In that bright eminence, and with his good
Upbraided none; nor was his service hard.   [45]
What could be less than to afford him praise,
The easiest recompense, and pay him thanks,
How due! Yet all his good proved ill in me,
And wrought but malice; lifted up so high
I 'sdained subjection, and thought one step higher   [50]
Would set me highest, and in a moment quit
The debt immense of endless gratitude,
So burdensome, still paying, still to owe;
Forgetful what from him I still received,
And understood not that a grateful mind   [55]
By owing owes not, but still pays, at once
Indebted and discharged; what burden then?
O had his powerful destiny ordained
Me some inferior angel, I had stood
Then happy; no unbounded hope had raised   [60]
Ambition. Yet why not? Some other Power
As great might have aspired, and me though mean
Drawn to his part; but other Powers as great
Fell not, but stand unshaken, from within
Or from without, to all temptations armed.   [65]
Hadst thou the same free will and power to stand?
Thou hadst: whom hast thou then or what to accuse,
But Heav'n's free love dealt equally to all?
But then his love accursed, since love or hate,
To me alike, it deals eternal woe.   [70]
Nay cursed be thou; since against his thy will

Chose freely what it now so justly rues.
Me miserable! Which way shall I fly
Infinite wrath, and infinite despair?
Which way I fly is Hell; myself am Hell;   [75]
And in the lowest deep a lower deep
Still threat'ning to devour me opens wide,
To which the Hell I suffer seems a Heav'n.
O then at last relent: is there no place
Left for repentance, none for pardon left?   [80]
None left but by submission; and that word
Disdain forbids me, and my dread of shame
Among the Spirits beneath, whom I seduced
With other promises and other vaunts
Than to submit, boasting I could subdue   [85]
Th' Omnipotent. Ay me, they little know
How dearly I abide that boast so vain,
Under what torments inwardly I groan;
While they adore me on the throne of Hell,
With diadem and scepter high advanced   [90]
The lower still I fall, only supreme
In misery; such joy ambition finds.
But say I could repent and could obtain
By act of grace my former state; how soon
Would heighth recall high thoughts, how soon unsay   [95]
What feigned submission swore: ease would recant
Vows made in pain, as violent and void.
For never can true reconcilement grow
Where wounds of deadly hate have pierced so deep:
Which would but lead me to a worse relapse   [100]
And heavier fall: so should I purchase dear
Short intermission bought with double smart.
This knows my punisher; therefore as far
From granting he, as I from begging peace:
All hope excluded thus, behold instead   [105]
Of us outcást, exíled, his new delight,
Mankind created, and for him this world.
So farewell hope, and with hope farewell fear,
Farewell remorse: all good to me is lost;
Evil be thou my good; by thee at least   [110]
Divided empire with Heav'n's King I hold
By thee, and more than half perhaps will reign;
As man ere long, and this new world shall know.
    Thus while he spake, each passion dimmed his face
Thrice changed with pale, ire, envy and despair,   [115]

Which marred his borrowed visage, and betrayed
Him counterfeit, if any eye beheld.
For Heav'nly minds from such distempers foul
Are ever clear. Whereof he soon aware,
Each perturbation smoothed with outward calm,   [120]
Artificer of fraud; and was the first
That practiced falsehood under saintly show,
Deep malice to conceal, couched with revenge:
Yet not enough had practiced to deceive
Uriel once warned; whose eye pursued him down   [125]
The way he went, and on th' Assyrian mount
Saw him disfigured, more than could befall
Spirit of happy sort: his gestures fierce
He marked and mad demeanor, then alone,
As he supposed, all unobserved, unseen.   [130]

4. Book IV. 356–92

This passage follows soon after the previous one and continues the same
ideas, but this time, Satan, now sitting on the tree of life in the Garden
of Eden disguised as a cormorant, reacts to having seen with us for the
first time Adam and Eve in their prelapsarian bliss (see passage 1 in the
paradise section below). The sight of the happy couple and the delights
of the garden move Satan to understandable rage and envy, but also
seem to stir in him feelings of 'mutual amity' (IV. 376) and impossible
happiness. It is as if Adam and Eve's state of innocence for a second
breaks through the relentless Calvinist despair of Satan and forces out
of him a self-contradictory speech, at once speaking of wonder and possible love but finally of woe, conquest, and of seeking with Adam and
Eve a 'league' (IV. 375) of the damned. This famous passage has often
divided critics who cannot decide if Satan is being for a moment sincere,
or if he is typically cynical and ironic throughout. What is certain,
however, is that if Satan is sincere in his initial thoughts of amity, the
sentiment prevails that with such friends, who needs enemies? In any
case, the good feeling does not last long, and despair soon catches up
with Satan. He finally contemplates Adam and Eve's future destruction
in a language which owes a profound debt to what Coleridge referred
to as Iago's 'motiveless malignity' in Shakespeare's *Othello*.[3] Satan, like
Iago, is motivated by pure hatred, but such consuming hatred can never
be a motive in any superficial causal sense; it is, rather, a destructive,
almost nihilistic emotive force stirred up from the 'bottom' of Satan's
despairing consciousness. This passage, together with the previous one,

thus completes the dramatisation of Satan's painfully reluctant assumption of his self-inflicted (but also in a sense predetermined) biblical role as humanity's arch-enemy. Whereas in the previous passage Milton uses theological language to dramatise Satan's despair, in this passage he turns to the language of Machiavellian realpolitik and New World conquest to dramatise his malice.

When Satan still in gaze, as first he stood,
Scarce thus at length failed speech recovered sad.
   O Hell! What do mine eyes with grief behold,
Into our room of bliss thus high advanced
Creatures of other mould, earth-born perhaps,   [360]
Not Spirits, yet to Heav'nly Spirits bright
Little inferior; whom my thoughts pursue
With wonder, and could love, so lively shines
In them divine resemblance, and such grace
The hand that formed them on their shape hath poured.   [365]
Ah gentle pair, ye little think how nigh
Your change approaches, when all these delights
Will vanish and deliver ye to woe,
More woe, the more your taste is now of joy;
Happy, but for so happy ill secured   [370]
Long to continue, and this high seat your Heav'n
Ill fenced for Heav'n to keep out such a foe
As now is entered; yet no purposed foe
To you whom I could pity thus forlorn
Though I unpitied: league with you I seek,   [375]
And mutual amity so strait, so close,
That I with you must dwell, or you with me
Henceforth; my dwelling haply may not please
Like this fair Paradise, your sense, yet such
Accept your Maker's work; he gave it me,   [380]
Which I as freely give; Hell shall unfold,
To entertain you two, her widest gates,
And send forth all her kings; there will be room,
Not like these narrow limits, to receive
Your numerous offspring; if no better place,   [385]
Thank him who puts me loath to this revenge
On you who wrong me not for him who wronged.
And should I at your harmless innocence
Melt, as I do, yet public reason just,
Honour and empire with revenge enlarged,   [390]
By conquering this new world, compels me now
To do what else though damned I should abhor.

Commentary and analysis

Concepts and themes

One of the main theological-philosophical themes which drive Milton's theodicy and the reimagining of hell and the fallen angels is the age-old quandary about how to explain the presence of evil in a world supposedly created perfect by an omnipotent good God. The paradox underlining the so-called 'problem of evil' in *Paradise Lost* was formulated in ancient times in Greek sceptical thought, and its most famous expression is widely (though perhaps wrongly) attributed to the Hellenistic materialist-atomist philosopher Epicurus, who was thought by the early Church Fathers, again wrongly, to be an atheist.[4] What has come to be known as the 'Epicurus' paradox states: if God is willing to prevent evil but is not able to, then he is not omnipotent. If he is able, but not willing, then he is himself evil. If he is both able and willing, then how can there be evil in the world? If he is neither able nor willing, then he is no God. This paradox dogged Judaeo-Christian theology from its inception, since both faiths hold that God is absolutely good and that He created the world according to His unconstrained and un-necessitated will and design, making it therefore a 'perfect' creation. A common, if perplexing, solution for this paradox proposed in both orthodox Judaism and most strands of Christianity is to suggest that evil is not in itself a created presence in the world, but is a consequence of sinfulness when the creature of God mars God's otherwise perfect creation through wilful sin. Broadly speaking, this was the orthodox Christian view upheld by St Augustine and later by St Thomas Aquinas as well. There are many possible consequences for holding such a view, but the one Milton clung to is that 'evil' is a negative quality left as a scar on divine creation when God, rejecting sinfulness, withdraws his goodness from parts of creation tainted by sin. Milton delights in the paradox. On the one hand God in creating hell, for example, necessarily created an evil place, but its evil is not a substantial attribute but a consequence of deprivation resulting from the absence of God's beatific presence. Milton's hell is a vacuous non-place within the 'boundless' deep, a 'universe of death' (II. 622), extrinsic to God and therefore antonymic to life and being itself.

Naturally, there are many contradictions and logical loopholes in this solution to the problem of evil, but its power from a position of faith is undeniable, especially as it is predicated necessarily on man having free will with which either to reject or embrace sin. Sin and evil become in this context the consequence of a misuse of free will, or a fundamental error in moral and spiritual judgement. Milton portrays evil coming into the world at the exact moment when Satan wilfully chooses to rebel against God. As we saw above (passage 2), the allegorical figure of Sin herself reminds Satan how after he manipulated a vast host of angels 'In bold conspiracy against Heav'n's King' (II. 751), she sprung from the left side of his head, 'a goddess armed' (II. 757), and soon won over the rebel angels with her 'attractive graces' (II. 762). Many readers might follow Empson in feeling that Milton plays the devil's advocate perhaps too persuasively in presenting Satan's choice as either inevitable and/or entirely just, but the poem as a whole consistently and systematically condemns such assessments, even as it raises their distinct rhetorical appeal, if not their logical plausibility. Milton follows orthodox Christianity in presenting Satan's sin as the sin of pride, but also, following Paul more specifically, as a sin of covetousness or wrong desire. Satan's sin is essentially Adam and Eve's sin writ large – the desire to 'be as gods, knowing good and evil' (Genesis 3: 5) and therefore morally self-reliant and independent from God the creator. From a theological point of view, Milton is entirely consistent in his portrayal of Satan's sinfulness as spiritually and morally devastating and as endemic of all acts of idolatry in the fallen world. Satan's sin leads to idolatry because it substitutes the worship due to God with the golden calf of self-worship and self-reliance. The hyphenated structure in *Paradise Lost* of adjectives and verbs consisting of the suffix 'self' reverberates throughout the poem as a mark of the idolater. In Book V (see passage 2 in the heaven section below) Raphael relates how leading up to the angelic rebellion in heaven, the obedient angel Abdiel admonished Satan by reminding him that angels could not presume to give law to God who created them, to which Satan replies by denying any memory of being created and raising the distinctly heretical possibility that 'We know no time when we were not as now; / Know none before us, self-begot, self-raised / By our own quick'ning power' (V. 859–61). This presumption is the root of all evil in *Paradise Lost*, and God says as much when earlier in Book III he uses the same construction to describe Satan and the rebel angels as 'Self-tempted, self-depraved' (III. 130).

From a literary point of view, Satan's character is a pastiche of mock-heroic Homeric grandeur, Machiavellian rhetorical power, and numerous vices and moral–theological errors. In creating Satan Milton drew on innumerable sources, but chiefly on the Bible and Apocrypha, the medieval morality 'vice' tradition, Shakespearean and Marlovian drama (especially *Othello*, *The Tempest* and *Dr Faustus*), and classical epic and mythology. The synthesis, however, is uniquely Milton's and the result is an imaginative tour de force. Milton's Satan is a protean figure whose image and consequent affective presence in the poem undergoes a gradual process of tragic degradation. Like a character from Ovid's *Metamorphoses* subject to numerous changes of form, Satan mutates in the poem from an awe-inspiring fallen angel, cut from the same cloth as Homer's Achilles or Virgil's Turnus, into a soliloquising Shakespearean Iago figure disguised as a cormorant, then into an ugly toad crouched by Eve's ear as she sleeps, whispering to her evil thoughts, and finally into a hissing, speechless serpent on whose head the Son will tread in final triumph at the end of days. This process of degradation corresponds to a diminution and flattening of Satan's substantial character, from the heights of Homeric heroism and depths of Shakespearean interiority to the theological embodiment of an evil archetype in the biblical symbol of the serpent. This movement of degradation is linked to the power of speech. Satan's presence in the poem, indeed his sense of character, is always a function of his rhetorical ability to tempt and deceive others, including and perhaps especially himself. The final insult of literally turning this magnificent character into the serpent of biblical prophecy is to see him deprived of his voice. Loss of speech and one's free rational agency associated with the ability to speak is the most terrible deprivation Milton could probably envision, and this is precisely why, as the angel Raphael says, the rebel angels' final punishment is eternal silence: 'Therefore eternal silence be their doom' (VI. 385).

Style and form
Satan's idolatrous evil is a function not just of what he says, but of how Milton has him say and unsay words that 'interwove with sighs' must find 'out their way' (I. 621) from his tormented mind. The principal quality of Satanic style in *Paradise Lost* is misdirection. It relies on the frequent use of what we might term today complex run-on sentences, inflated periods riddled with oxymora and paradox, and chiastic rhetorical structures in which a sentence meanders through a maze of double negatives and reversals. A good example is the opening words of Satan to Beelzebub (passage 1 above):

> into what pit thou seest
> From what heighth fall'n, so much the stronger proved
> He with his thunder: and till then who knew
> The force of those dire arms? yet not for those,
> Nor what the potent Victor in his rage
> Can else inflict, do I repent or change,

Though changed in outward lustre, that fixed mind
And high disdain, from sense of injured merit,
That with the mightiest raised me to contend
(I. 91–9)

The unusual word order of these lines does much more than create
a magniloquent effect; it serves a rhetorical purpose. Satan, here as
elsewhere, is attempting to downplay the extreme transgression of his
rebellion and the eternity of the punishment he himself later concedes
to be just. The effect, while dazzling, is also self-contradictory. Satan's
rhetoric constantly seeks to diminish God ('He with his thunder') in
portraying the failed angelic rebellion as a battle lost between weaker
and stronger foes. Such a plainly absurd claim as 'till then who knew /
The force of those dire arms?', pretending ignorance of God's omnipotence, nevertheless sounds persuasive because of its sonorous dignity
and because Satan's 'sense of injured merit' finds expression in emotively
powerful language: if Satan *feels* so strongly about what he has to say,
then surely he is in some measure justified in feeling this way. However,
persuasive though Satan's rhetoric may be it continually founders on its
own conceits. Words like 'stronger', 'force', and 'potent', when detached
from each other in separate clauses, do suggest a degree of power relative to that clause, but as the sentence gathers momentum such words
accumulate to suggest precisely the omnipotence Satan hopes to obscure.
The move from the comparative 'stronger' to the superlative 'mightiest'
towards the end of the sentence gives the impression that Satan is not
quite in command of his argument. The result is contradiction. Satan
claims to have a 'fixed mind', elsewhere translated in the poem into an
attempt to borrow Stoic concepts of mental strength in the face of adver-
sity. But the chiastic structure of the clause which precedes it, 'Nor . . .
do I repent or change, / Though changed in outward lustre', unhinges
any notion of fixity Satan can pretend to. Although Satan claims to have
changed only in outer form, the language Milton writes for him betrays
a duplicitous, shifty personality emptied of a moral centre and therefore
subject now to *constant* change.

The unique style of hell, with its sense of eviscerated materiality, also
extends in the poem to the use of negative and proleptic epic similes
associated with Satan and the devils. In hell, Milton's epic similes complement the devils' fallen rhetoric in enhancing the sense of loss and
dread which attends them. One of the most famous and most beautiful
of these similes likens the prone Satan, lying on the burning lake, to a
monstrous sea beast (passage 1):

his other parts besides
Prone on the flood, extended long and large
Lay floating many a rood, in bulk as huge
As whom the fables name of monstrous size,
Titanian, or Earth-born, that warred on Jove,
Briareos or Typhon, whom the den
By ancient Tarsus held, or that sea-beast
Leviathan, which God of all his works
Created hugest that swim th' Océan stream:
Him haply slumb'ring on the Norway foam
The pilot of some small night-foundered skiff,
Deeming some island, oft, as seamen tell,
With fixèd anchor in his scaly rind
Moors by his side under the lee, while night
Invests the sea, and wishèd morn delays
(I. 194–208)

The first striking thing to note about this simile is its equivocation, a common strategy of Milton's. The usual correspondence required of a simile where x is like y is undermined here by the open-ended formula of x is like y, *or* w, *or* z. Satan's shifty indeterminacy spills in this case into the simile itself so that even as the simile heaps up associations on the literal situation of Satan lying prone on a lake of fire – associations of rebellion and hubris (the Titan Briareos), of deception and affliction (the Leviathan of the Book of Job), and possibly of Catholic idolatry (Fowler's comment on 'prone' and 'rood') – these associations cannot grasp a single point of central correspondence that might anchor the essence of Satan's evil. The simile is also loose in another way, since only the final image of a whale actually corresponds to the situation which sparked the simile to begin with. Significantly, the final image of the whale ends the simile with the image of an anchor. As the simile expands, Satan is likened to a whale in the North Sea whose back, peering above the waves, is mistaken by 'the pilot of some small night-foundered skiff' for a solid island onto which he latches with a 'fixed anchor'. In shifting focus from the whale to the seaman in his fragile boat, the simile by this stage is no longer about Satan, but about the reader's perception of Satan. The reader is drawn into the simile through the image of the 'pilot' who mistakes Satan's evil, lurking beneath the surface, for the sheltering solidity of an island. The word 'fixed' picks up, moreover, the illusion of Satan's 'fixed mind' earlier in the passage and has the exact opposite effect of un-mooring the reader's possibly misguided assumptions about Satan's heroism.

Historical-political context

Satan's heroic grandeur in the opening books is not just misleading ethically but also politically and biographically. What is the reader to do with the knowledge that Milton, like Satan, was a rebel who sided with those who dethroned and executed an anointed monarch? Is not that precisely what Satan tries to do in *Paradise Lost*? Once again, the reader is led into an interpretative hall of mirrors. As discussed in Chapter 1, Milton did not object to the idea of monarchy but to the idea of tyranny, and the question that readers must ask themselves is who the real tyrant is, God or Satan? In this respect careful reading, not even between the lines, indicates that Satan is clearly a tyrant of the worst kind. His followers are not loyal to him out of respect and rational admiration, but out of 'dread' and slavish degeneration, fawning and bowing to him 'With awful reverence prone; and as a god / Extol him equal to the highest in Heav'n' (II. 478–9). Moreover, the council of devils Satan presides over in Book II, sitting like a decadent Asiatic Sultan (or perhaps a Stuart king?) 'High on a throne of royal state, which far / Outshone the wealth of Ormus and of Ind' (II. 1–2), is a mockery of free debate. What ensues is a superficially democratic assembly in which various speakers propose courses of action, in what is in fact a rehearsed exercise meant to legitimise Satan's continuing leadership of the devilish host. There is no real freedom of debate in this hellish council, certainly not of the pious, rational kind Milton elsewhere extolled. When Satan congratulates the devils on their democratic proceedings and says, 'Well have ye judged, well ended long debate, / Synod of gods' (II. 390–1), the modern reader may well think of certain modern-day dictatorships where rigged elections held under the gun yield 100 per cent of the votes to the only candidate. Milton, however, had other democratic assemblies in mind, including those synods of Presbyterians, Parliamentary assemblies, and the republican Council of State (under whose government Milton was employed), which lapsed into tyranny in different ways after the creation of the republic. The council in hell is not a mock democracy, but an exploration of the mockery *of* democracy.

However, that Satan is a tyrant does not yet exonerate an absolutist God from a similar charge. As always in *Paradise Lost*, Milton allows for multiple and often contradictory possible readings to compete for the reader's attention, so that the political allegory which emerges from the opening books is decidedly an ambiguous one. Sharon Achinstein has shown that in depicting Satan and the devils in council Milton relies on imagery and tropes bearing very close resemblance to the 'Parliament of Hell' genre used by royalists and anti-Cromwellians to denounce the

Interregnum parliament as diabolic. Was Milton then voicing royalist ideas in an effort to appease his many enemies after the Restoration? Or was he perhaps attempting to register his own personal disgust with the republican revolutionaries who lost their way? These questions are not made any easier when we note that Milton's Satan uses the republican language of a rebel fighting the alleged tyranny of 'he who reigns / Monarch in Heav'n' (I. 637–8). This raises the possible view that Satan, like Cromwell and the republican leaders, only *lapsed* into tyranny but that the cause for which he fought was still very much one in spirit with the 'Good Old Cause' of English republican aspirations, and therefore entirely just. This idea, however, does not bear scrutiny since it once again depends on false (Satanic) logic, which confuses the metaphorical with the literal and flattens the monistic hierarchy that Milton's theodicy in the poem otherwise depends on. Satan represents a double idolatry and tyranny in that he embodies the political abuses of *both* the Stuart kings *and* the republican leaders, both of whom in Milton's final analysis betrayed the English people before God. In Milton's view, a king or a lord protector does not govern by divine right, but as a deputy of God who must be held to account if they betray their sacred office. What God is absolutely, men can only be in a borrowed, deputed manner. God's monarchy is universal, a priori and unassailable, and he can only ever be a tyrant if he is no longer in any meaningful sense God. Of course, one of the charges laid against Milton's poem is that in portraying God as a character he precisely lowers him to such a level that readers might think of him as a tyrant and any political analogy is fair play, but as we will see in the next section, here too things are not as straightforward as they initially seem.

Heaven, God and theodicy

If Satan is the most deceptively pleasing character of the epic, God has to be, unintentionally, its least pleasing character for the simple reason that he *is* a character. Representations of God in one form or another were not uncommon in art and literature before *Paradise Lost*, but Milton's speaking God and the representation of heaven more generally constitute a radical departure from any artistic or literary Christian convention before its time. No one, not Dante in the *Commedia* and not even Du Bartas, whose religious epic poem about the seven days of creation Milton admired, presumed to assume God's direct point of view in quite the same way as Milton. Milton's literary audacity is even more extraordinary when we consider that for Protestants following in the teachings of Luther and Calvin, the hidden God portrayed in the Hebrew Bible was a mysterious figure of power and majesty from whom man has been utterly divorced by sin. The majority of Protestants were taught to believe that fallen man could only hope to approach this angry, inscrutable deity through the mediatory office of the incarnated Christ, the Word made flesh. However, in wanting to present God's judgement of fallen man as logically and even legally cogent, Milton had to go against these conventions and allow for a literary persona of God to pronounce his providential justice directly to the reader in lucid, declarative language. This move may have been necessary from a logical, didactic perspective, but it is also in one sense counter-productive. Once the reader realises that they are being lectured to in the poem not by God, but only by a presumptuous human poet assuming God's point of view, it is very difficult to accept the theology while resisting the very human urge to argue. Curiously, however, it seems that Milton *does* want us to argue. Or, to put it more precisely, Milton wants us to engage with the argument, work out its reasoning and possible contradictions, and come to terms in the process with our redemptive potential as rational, though fallen, human beings. Milton's God deliberately confronts the reader not with an inadvertent paradox about the impossibility of conceptualising God in art, but with the essential paradox underlying all flawed, human perceptions of deity.

If Milton's Satan is meant to tempt us and draw us in, therefore, Milton's God is meant to perplex us and define the limits within which our reasoning must operate. However, in the battle for the reader's sympathy Satan has an unfair advantage. Most readers, apparently even readers with no religious inclination whatsoever, are willing to accept that Satan might have relatable interiority and depth, but feel uncomfortable in allowing for even a slight hint of similar complexity in God. When Milton's God speaks as a character in the poem the loss of mystery such speech entails can be devastating to how readers react to the content of the speeches. This is not a matter of religious propriety, but of literary plausibility which the paradox of God's traditional remoteness deeply problematises. God is meant to be inscrutable, mysterious and certainly not human, so that the process of literary presentation necessarily diminishes God; by presenting God as a being who acts in time and expresses himself in linear syntax and causal logic Milton's God becomes, by definition, a finite being. A possible defence against these charges might reply that in fact Milton's God has no interiority to speak of in the poem, and that it is even questionable whether he is a character at all in the conventional literary sense. Even at his most accessible, Milton's God is a disembodied voice speaking to us from the other side of absolute divine alterity and transcendence, his glory shrouded in darkness. Milton impossibly wants his readers to accept that the vision of heaven is accommodated to our fallen perceptions, and therefore not to be read literally, but also to accept that *what* God speaks in this accommodated manner is nevertheless literally true from a divine point of view. This move finally requires that the reader accept Milton's created God as an expression of Milton's prophetic authority in the poem. This effectively creates a split between Milton's created God and the truly transcendental God hovering on the metaphysical edge of Milton's art – the God hailed by the angels in their hymn in Book III as 'omnipotent, / Immutable, immortal, infinite . . . thyself invisible / Amidst the glorious brightness where thou sitt'st / Throned inaccessible' (III. 372–7).

Finally, however, readers should always bear in mind that Milton's project of theodicy depends on the cumulative didactic effect of the poem as a whole, not just on those moments in the poem when God speaks his mind. Readers who only note the inevitable diminution of God without noting the many strategies Milton deploys in the poem to reverse this diminution are at best uncharitable, and at worst 'of the devil's party'. Milton's literary representation of heaven and the angelic proximity with God constantly self-references its imagined artificiality and biblical conventionality from a fallen perspective. The entire sequence of the heavenly council where the Father speaks with the Son is conducted under the inspired narrator's accommodated vision, where Milton concedes and reminds us that the limits of art have not been transgressed but only temporarily obscured in the interests of his 'great argument'. Moreover, the representation of heaven and divine speech in *Paradise Lost* depends not just on the clarity of logic, but on the deepness of emotional affect as well, and on literary strategies which encode the reader's experience of loss and regret so central to Milton's theodicy throughout the poem. As we have seen with Satan and will see again with Adam and Eve, theodicy is not just a function in the poem of abstract theology, but of the dramatic points of view through which its abstractions are filtered. In this respect, Milton's heavenly perspective continually mirrors and inverts the satanic perspective with which the poem opens, and the two inverted perspectives we soon learn are interdependent. After dragging the reader through hell in Books I and II Milton lifts us up to heaven in Book III, as he soars from the paradox of hell's 'darkness visible' (I. 63) to the inverse paradox of heaven's 'unapproachèd light' (III. 4). But as we move with

Milton from one impossible vision into another, up into the imagined heavenly vision 'Of things invisible to mortal sight' (III. 55), we carry with us as a dark presence the satanic perspective we acquired in the opening books and it taints our reading of heaven with scorn. Equally, having read through Books III–VIII, we might then feel encouraged to reread Books I and II with a measure of divine light now correcting the earlier satanic perspective, and again moving forward in the narrative, bring both perspectives to bear on our reading of the tragic events of the Fall in Books IX–X. The satanic and divine perspectives continually compete for our attention, and one view always undermines the other. Milton's God may very well be a flawed literary creation, but the poem constantly reminds us that the flaws are always relative to our own necessarily fallen point of view.

Key passages

1. Book III. 56–343
In terms of narrative progression, Book III follows seamlessly from Book II, but the perspective changes radically. At the end of Book II we saw Satan emerging from hell and the gulf of chaos, heading towards 'This pendent world' (II. 1052) and the sun. But as Satan makes his journey, in cinematic terms we might say that the camera pans up and away above him into heaven, as we see the figure of Satan, ever smaller, from God's omniscient point of view. The epic narrator acts as our 'camera' and affects these shifts of perspective on our behalf. After the opening invocation to 'holy Light' (III. 1) and a guarded disclaimer which concedes that the sights we are about to see are in fact forbidden to reveal to mere mortals, we are brought into the presence of God himself, sitting 'throned above all heighth' (III. 58), commenting to his Son sitting next to him on the sight of the rebel Satan 'Coasting the wall of Heav'n on this side Night / In the dun air sublime' (III. 71–2). The anthropomorphism of the scene may be distasteful to some, but it is finally balanced by a sense of God's timelessness and majestic power; while God may well be trapped with us in a single narrative moment, he nevertheless speaks 'from his prospect high, / Wherein past, present, future he beholds' (III. 77–8). What ensues is one of the most important dialogues in the poem, in which God the Father, 'foreseeing' (III. 79) the events of the Fall, sets out very clearly the theology of free will and obedience on which the logical case for the justification of his ways to men depends (III. 80–134). Having set out his decree of free will, the Father then pronounces his judgement, condemning man to death unless 'for

him / Some other able, and as willing, pay / The rigid satisfaction, death for death' (III. 210–12). At that moment the Son volunteers to redeem man and atone for his sin (III. 227–65), as the jubilant Father accepts the Son's offer. The so-called 'council in heaven', which mirrors all too uncomfortably the mock-democratic council of the devils earlier in Book II, finally then concludes with the Son's and the Father's respective apocalyptic visions of the Second Coming and Judgement Day.

Theologically speaking, the Father's resonantly Arminian opening speech and subsequent discussion of grace are crucial for an understanding of the poem's overarching argument. Milton puts into the mouth of God a speech which contains key theological ideas about human free will and moral agency, chief of which is the idea, as God says, that he created man 'just and right, / Sufficient to have stood, though free to fall' (III. 98–9), and that Adam and Eve are consequently 'authors to themselves in all / Both what they judge and what they choose' (III. 122–3). This speech, however, is also one of the most controversial in the poem. As will be discussed in the commentary section below, the theology is in places inevitably flawed logically and is constantly undermined by the literary conventions framing it. God's detached aloofness at key moments gives way to what reads like outbursts of human emotion unbecoming of God, and the suspiciously anti-Trinitarian subordination which dominates the relationship of the Father to the Son in this passage potentially empties the emerging theology of the atonement from its traditional association with the Christian message of unconditional divine love. Divorced from the Son's voluntary mercy, the Father's love is anything but unconditional, while his demand of a 'rigid satisfaction' is potentially far too legalistic and cold for most Christian readers to bear. However, as will also be shown below, such criticism is mostly unfair. It overlooks the dramatic aim of the sequence as a whole, and the possibility that what triumphs in the end is the heavenly council's didactic and affective impact on the reader's ability to process the enormity of the Fall in moral and existential terms.

> Now had th' Almighty Father from above,
> From the pure Empyrean where he sits
> High throned above all heighth, bent down his eye,
> His own works and their works at once to view:
> About him all the sanctities of Heaven   [60]
> Stood thick as stars, and from his sight received
> Beatitude past utterance; on his right
> The radiant image of his glory sat,
> His only Son; on earth he first beheld

Our two first parents, yet the only two   [65]
Of mankind, in the happy garden placed,
Reaping immortal fruits of joy and love,
Uninterrupted joy, unrivalled love
In blissful solitude; he then surveyed
Hell and the gulf between, and Satan there   [70]
Coasting the wall of Heav'n on this side Night
In the dun air sublime, and ready now
To stoop with wearied wings, and willing feet
On the bare outside of this world, that seemed
Firm land imbosomed without firmament,   [75]
Uncertain which, in ocean or in air.
Him God beholding from his prospect high,
Wherein past, present, future he beholds,
Thus to his only Son foreseeing spake.

    Only begotten Son, seest thou what rage   [80]
Transports our Adversary, whom no bounds
Prescribed, no bars of Hell, nor all the chains
Heaped on him there, nor yet the main abyss
Wide interrupt can hold; so bent he seems
On desperate revenge, that shall redound   [85]
Upon his own rebellious head. And now
Through all restraint broke loose he wings his way
Not far off Heav'n, in the precincts of light,
Directly towards the new created world,
And man there placed, with purpose to assay   [90]
If him by force he can destroy, or worse,
By some false guile pervert; and shall pervert;
For men will hearken to his glozing lies,
And easily transgress the sole command,
Sole pledge of his obedience: so will fall   [95]
He and his faithless progeny: whose fault?
Whose but his own? Ingrate, he had of me
All he could have; I made him just and right,
Sufficient to have stood, though free to fall.
Such I created all th' ethereal Powers   [100]
And Spirits, both them who stood and them who failed;
Freely they stood who stood, and fell who fell.
Not free, what proof could they have giv'n sincere
Of true allegiance, constant faith or love,
Where only what they needs must do, appeared,   [105]
Not what they would? What praise could they receive?
What pleasure I from such obedience paid,
When will and reason (reason also is choice)

Useless and vain, of freedom both despoiled,
Made passive both, had served necessity,   [110]
Not me. They therefore as to right belonged,
So were created, nor can justly accuse
Their Maker, or their making, or their fate,
As if predestination overruled
Their will, disposed by absolute decree   [115]
Or high foreknowledge; they themselves decreed
Their own revolt, not I: if I foreknew,
Foreknowledge had no influence on their fault,
Which had no less proved certain unforeknown.
So without least impúlse or shadow of Fate,   [120]
Or aught by me immutably foreseen,
They trespass, authors to themselves in all
Both what they judge and what they choose; for so
I formed them free, and free they must remain,
Till they enthrall themselves: I else must change   [125]
Their nature, and revoke the high decree
Unchangeable, eternal, which ordained
Their freedom; they themselves ordained their Fall.
The first sort by their own suggestion fell,
Self-tempted, self-depraved: man falls deceived   [130]
By the other first: man therefore shall find grace;
The other none: in mercy and justice both,
Through Heav'n and earth, so shall my glory excel,
But mercy first and last shall brightest shine.
      Thus while God spake, ambrosial fragrance filled   [135]
All Heav'n, and in the blessèd Spirits elect
Sense of new joy ineffable diffused:
Beyond compare the Son of God was seen
Most glorious, in him all his Father shone
Substantially expressed, and in his face   [140]
Divine compassion visibly appeared,
Love without end, and without measure grace,
Which uttering thus he to his Father spake.
      O Father, gracious was that word which closed
Thy sov'reign sentence, that man should find grace;   [145]
For which both Heav'n and earth shall high extol
Thy praises, with th' innumerable sound
Of hymns and sacred songs, wherewith thy throne
Encompassed shall resound thee ever blest.
For should man finally be lost, should man   [150]
Thy creature late so loved, thy youngest son
Fall circumvented thus by fraud, though joined

With his own folly? That be from thee far,
That far be from thee, Father, who art judge
Of all things made, and judgest only right.   [155]
Or shall the Adversary thus obtain
His end, and frustrate thine, shall he fulfil
His malice, and thy goodness bring to naught,
Or proud return though to his heavier doom,
Yet with revenge accomplished and to Hell   [160]
Draw after him the whole race of mankind,
By him corrupted? Or wilt thou thyself
Abolish thy creation, and unmake,
For him, what for thy glory thou hast made?
So should thy goodness and thy greatness both   [165]
Be questioned and blasphemed without defence.
      To whom the great Creator thus replied.
O Son, in whom my soul hath chief delight,
Son of my bosom, Son who art alone
My Word, my wisdom, and effectual might,   [170]
All hast thou spoken as my thoughts are, all
As my eternal purpose hath decreed:
Man shall not quite be lost, but saved who will,
Yet not of will in him, but grace in me
Freely vouchsafed; once more I will renew   [175]
His lapsèd powers, though forfeit and enthralled
By sin to foul exorbitant desires;
Upheld by me, yet once more he shall stand
On even ground against his mortal foe,
By my upheld, that he may know how frail   [180]
His fall'n condition is, and to me owe
All his deliverance, and to none but me.
Some I have chosen of peculiar grace
Elect above the rest; so is my will:
The rest shall hear me call, and oft be warned   [185]
Their sinful state, and to appease betimes
Th' incensèd Deity, while offered grace
Invites; for I will clear their senses dark,
What may suffice, and soften stony hearts
To pray, repent, and bring obedience due.   [190]
To prayer, repentance, and obedience due,
Though but endeavoured with sincere intent,
Mine ear shall not be slow, mine eye not shut.
And I will place within them as a guide
My umpire conscience, whom if they will hear,   [195]
Light after light well-used they shall attain,

And to the end persisting, safe arrive.
This my long sufferance and my day of grace
They who neglect and scorn, shall never taste;
But hard be hardened, blind be blinded more,   [200]
That they may stumble on, and deeper fall;
And none but such from mercy I exclude.
But yet all is not done; man disobeying,
Disloyal breaks his fealty, and sins
Against the high supremacy of Heav'n,   [205]
Affecting Godhead, and so losing all,
To expiate his treason hath naught left,
But to destruction sacred and devote,
He with his whole posterity must die,
Die he or Justice must; unless for him   [210]
Some other able, and as willing, pay
The rigid satisfaction, death for death.
Say Heav'nly Powers, where shall we find such love,
Which of ye will be mortal to redeem
Man's mortal crime, and just th' unjust to save,   [215]
Dwells in all Heaven charity so dear?
      He asked, but all the Heav'nly choir stood mute,
And silence was in Heav'n: on man's behalf
Patron or intercessor none appeared,
Much less that durst upon his own head draw   [220]
The deadly forfeiture, and ransom set.
And now without redemption all mankind
Must have been lost, adjudged to death and Hell
By doom severe, had not the Son of God,
In whom the fullness dwells of love divine,   [225]
His dearest meditation thus renewed.
      Father, thy word is past, man shall find grace;
And shall grace not find means, that finds her way,
The speediest of thy wingèd messengers,
To visit all thy creatures, and to all   [230]
Comes unprevented, unimplored, unsought,
Happy for man, so coming; he her aid
Can never seek, once dead in sins and lost;
Atonement for himself or offering meet,
Indebted and undone, hath none to bring: [235]
Behold me then, me for him, life for life
I offer, on me let thine anger fall;
Account me man; I for his sake will leave
Thy bosom, and this glory next to thee
Freely put off, and for him lastly die   [240]

Well pleased, on me let Death wreck all his rage;
Under his gloomy power I shall not long
Lie vanquished; thou hast given me to possess
Life in myself for ever, by thee I live,
Though now to Death I yield, and am his due   [245]
All that of me can die, yet that debt paid,
Thou wilt not leave me in the loathsome grave
His prey, nor suffer my unspotted soul
For ever with corruption there to dwell;
But I shall rise victorious, and subdue   [250]
My vanquisher, spoiled of his vaunted spoil;
Death his death's wound shall then receive, and stoop
Inglorious, of his mortal sting disarmed.
I through the ample air in triumph high
Shall lead Hell captive maugre Hell, and show   [255]
The powers of darkness bound. Thou at the sight
Pleased, out of Heaven shalt look down and smile,
While by thee raised I ruin all my foes,
Death last, and with his carcass glut the grave:
Then with the multitude of my redeemed   [260]
Shall enter Heaven long absent, and return,
Father, to see thy face, wherein no cloud
Of anger shall remain, but peace assured,
And reconcilement; wrath shall be no more
Thenceforth, but in thy presence joy entire.   [265]
        His words here ended, but his meek aspéct
Silent yet spake, and breathed immortal love
To mortal men, above which only shone
Filial obedience: as a sacrifice
Glad to be offered, he attends the will   [270]
Of his great Father. Admiration seized
All Heav'n, what this might mean, and whither tend
Wond'ring; but soon th' Almighty thus replied:
        O thou in Heav'n and earth the only peace
Found out for mankind under wrath, O thou   [275]
My sole complacence! Well thou know'st how dear
To me are all my works, nor man the least
Though last created, that for him I spare
Thee from my bosom and right hand, to save,
By losing thee a while, the whole race lost.   [280]
Thou therefore whom thou only canst redeem,
Their nature also to thy nature join;
And be thyself man among men on earth,
Made flesh, when time shall be, of virgin seed,

By wondrous birth: be thou in Adam's room   [285]
The head of all mankind, though Adam's son.
As in him perish all men, so in thee
As from a second root shall be restored,
As many as are restored, without thee none.
His crime makes guilty all his sons; thy merit   [290]
Imputed shall absolve them who renounce
Their own both righteous and unrighteous deeds,
And live in thee transplanted, and from thee
Receive new life. So man, as is most just,
Shall satisfy for man, be judged and die,   [295]
And dying rise, and rising with him raise
His brethren, ransomed with his own dear life.
So Heav'nly love shall outdo Hellish hate,
Giving to death, and dying to redeem,
So dearly to redeem what Hellish hate   [300]
So easily destroyed, and still destroys
In those who, when they may, accept not grace.
Nor shalt thou by descending to assume
Man's nature, lessen or degrade thine own.
Because thou hast, though throned in highest bliss   [305]
Equal to God, and equally enjoying
God-like fruition, quitted all to save
A world from utter loss, and hast been found
By merit more than birthright Son of God,
Found worthiest to be so by being good,   [310]
Far more than great or high; because in thee
Love hath abounded more than glory abounds,
Therefore thy humiliation shall exalt
With thee thy manhood also to this throne;
Here shalt thou sit incarnate, here shalt reign   [315]
Both God and man, Son both of God and man,
Anointed universal King; all power
I give thee, reign for ever, and assume
Thy merits; under thee as Head Supreme
Thrones, Princedoms, Powers, Dominions I reduce: [320]
All knees to thee shall bow, of them that bide
In Heaven, or earth, or under earth in Hell;
When thou attended gloriously from Heav'n
Shalt in the sky appear, and from thee send
The summoning Archangels to proclaim   [325]
Thy dread tribunal: forthwith from all winds
The living, and forthwith the cited dead
Of all past ages to the general doom

Shall hasten, such a peal shall rouse their sleep.
Then all thy saints assembled, thou shalt judge   [330]
Bad men and angels, they arraigned shall sink
Beneath thy sentence; Hell, her numbers full,
Thenceforth shall be for ever shut. Meanwhile
The world shall burn, and from her ashes spring
New heav'n and earth, wherein the just shall dwell,   [335]
And after all their tribulations long
See golden days, fruitful of golden deeds,
With joy and love triúmphing, and fair truth.
Then thou thy regal sceptre shalt lay by,
For regal sceptre then no more shall need,   [340]
God shall be All in All. But all ye gods,
Adore him, who to compass all this dies,
Adore the Son, and honour him as me.

2. Book V. 743–907

In the course of Book V, God 'to render man inexcusable sends Raphael to admonish him of his obedience, of his free estate, of his enemy near at hand; who he is, and why his enemy, and whatever else may avail Adam to know' ('The Argument' to Book V). Raphael's lecture offers Adam and Eve (as well as the reader eavesdropping on the conversation) a glimpse into events in heaven which led to the angelic rebellion prior to the creation of the world. We thus hear how, at a point outside created earthly time, God declared to all the assembled angels, 'This day I have begot whom I declare / My only Son, and on this holy hill / Him have anointed, whom ye now behold / At my right hand' (V. 603–6). This, as historians might say, is the cause of all the trouble that next ensues. Satan, until then the pre-eminent archangel in heaven's hierarchy, feels slighted by the elevation of the upstart 'Son' and leads a host of 'innumerable' (V. 745) angels in rebellion against the alleged tyranny of God. In the passage below, taken from the end of Book V, Raphael relates how Satan began to stir up this host of gathered rebel angels with a rhetorically seductive yet typically contradictory speech, but met with fierce resistance from a single faithful angel, Abdiel, whose Hebrew name means 'servant of God'. The Satan–Abdiel exchange is one of the most famous and much-discussed passages in the poem, not least because it raises many problems of interpretation. Most critics agree, for example, that here for the first time in the poem we actually witness the precise moment when Satan falls, either in presuming to set himself up as God on his own mock 'Mount of Congregation', or more decisively in denying having been created by God in the first place.

However, as Empson pointed out, Satan's denial of his divine created-ness follows its own strong interior logic in objecting to the seemingly arbitrary elevation of the Son as somehow superior to the other angels in creation. After all, it is not at all obvious that angels would remember being created unless they were told so or could intuit it. Satan's denial of his creation may be utterly blasphemous in our eyes, but then Abdiel's confident knowledge to the contrary has no support *within* the poem itself.[5] Equally, the same political-contextual ambiguities which we encountered with Satan's republican language in Books I–II continue to confuse us here. Satan the demagogue again (but actually for the first time from a sequential narrative point of view) falls back on the republican discourse of liberty, while Abdiel the 'fervent angel' (V. 849) – a thinly disguised post-revolutionary Milton, 'Among the faithless, faithful only he' (V. 897) – zealously defends the absolutism of God's monarchy. Abdiel's ripostes to Satan's rhetorical flourishes are couched in equally polemical language which subtly subverts Satan's republican harangue and restates Milton's central antinomian teachings about obedient freedom as opposed to mere anarchy and license masquerading as liberty.

> So spake the Son, but Satan with his powers
> Far was advanced on wingèd speed, an host
> Innumerable as the stars of night,   [745]
> Or stars of morning, dew-drops, which the sun
> Impearls on every leaf and every flow'r.
> Regions they passed, the mighty regencies
> Of Seraphim and Potentates and Thrones
> In their triple degrees, regions to which   [750]
> All thy dominion, Adam, is no more
> Than what this garden is to all the earth,
> And all the sea, from one entire globose
> Stretched into longitude; which having passed
> At length into the limits of the North   [755]
> They came, and Satan to his royal seat
> High on a hill, far blazing, as a mount
> Raised on a mount, with pyramids and tow'rs
> From diamond quarries hewn, and rocks of gold,
> The palace of great Lucifer, (so call   [760]
> That structure in the dialect of men
> Interpreted) which not long after, he
> Affecting all equality with God,
> In imitation of that Mount whereon
> Messiah was declared in sight of Heav'n,   [765]

The Mountain of the Congregation called;
For thither he assembled all his train,
Pretending so commanded to consult
About the great reception of their King,
Thither to come, and with calumnious art   [770]
Of counterfeited truth thus held their ears.
    Thrones, Dominations, Princedoms, Virtues, Powers,
If these magnific titles yet remain
Not merely titular, since by decree
Another now hath to himself engrossed   [775]
All power, and us eclipsed under the name
Of King anointed, for whom all this haste
Of midnight march, and hurried meeting here,
This only to consult how we may best
With what may be devised of honours new   [780]
Receive him coming to receive from us
Knee-tribute yet unpaid, prostration vile,
Too much to one, but double how endured,
To one and to his image now proclaimed?
But what if better counsels might erect   [785]
Our minds and teach us to cast off this yoke?
Will ye submit your necks, and choose to bend
The supple knee? ye will not, if I trust
To know ye right, of if ye know yourselves
Natives and sons of Heav'n possessed before   [790]
By none, and if not equal all, yet free,
Equally free; for orders and degrees
Jar not with liberty, but well consist.
Who can in reason then or right assume
Monarchy over such as live by right   [795]
His equals, if in power and splendour less,
In freedom equal? or can introduce
Law and edíct on us, who without law
Err not, much less for this to be our Lord,
And look for adoration to th' abuse   [800]
Of those imperial titles which assert
Our being ordained to govern, not to serve?
    Thus far his bold discourse without control
Had audience, when among the Seraphim
Abdiel, than whom none with more zeal adored   [805]
The Deity, and divine commands obeyed,
Stood up, and in a flame of zeal severe
The current of his fury thus opposed.
    O argument blasphémous, false and proud!

Words which no ear ever to hear in Heav'n   [810]
Expected, least of all from thee, ingrate
In place thyself so high above your peers.
Canst thou with impious obloquy condemn
The just decree of God, pronounced and sworn,
That to his only Son by right endued   [815]
With regal sceptre, every soul in Heav'n
Shall bend the knee, and in that honour due
Confess him rightful King? unjust thou say'st
Flatly unjust, to bind with laws the free,
And equal over equals to let reign,   [820]
One over all with unsucceeded power.
Shalt thou give law to God, shalt thou dispute
With him the points of liberty, who made
Thee what thou art, and formed the Powers of Heav'n
Such as he pleased, and circumscribed their being?   [825]
Yet by experience taught we know how good,
And of our good, and of our dignity
How provident he is, how far from thought
To make us less, bent rather to exalt
Our happy state under one head more near   [830]
United. But to grant it thee unjust,
That equal over equals monarch reign:
Thyself though great and glorious dost thy count,
Or all angelic nature joined in one,
Equal to him begotten Son, by whom   [835]
As by his Word the mighty Father made
All things, ev'n thee, and all the Spirits of Heav'n
By him created in their bright degrees,
Crowned them with glory, and to their glory named,
Thrones, Dominations, Princedoms, Virtues, Powers,   [840]
Essential Powers, nor by his reign obscured,
But more illustrious made, since he the head
One of our number thus reduced becomes,
His laws our laws, all honour to him done
Returns our own. Cease then this impious rage,   [845]
And tempt not these; but hasten to appease
Th' incensèd Father, and th' incensèd Son,
While pardon may be found in time besought.
        So spake the fervent angel, but his zeal
None seconded, as out of season judged,   [850]
Or singular and rash, whereat rejoiced
Th' Apostate, and more haughty thus replied.
That we were formed then say'st thou? and the work

Of secondary hands, by task transferred
From Father to his Son? strange point and new!   [855]
Doctrine which we would know whence learnt: who saw
When this creation was? remember'st thou
Thy making, while the Maker gave thee being?
We know no time when we were not as now;
Know none before us, self-begot, self-raised   [860]
By our own quick'ning power, when fatal course
Had circled his full orb, the birth mature
Of this our native Heav'n, ethereal sons.
Our puissance is our own, our own right hand
Shall teach us highest deeds, by proof to try   [865]
Who is our equal: then thou shalt behold
Whether by supplication we intend
Address, and to begirt th' Almighty throne
Beseeching or besieging. This report,
These tidings carry to th' anointed King;   [870]
And fly, ere evil intercept thy flight.
       He said, and as the sound of waters deep
Hoarse murmur echoed to his words applause
Through the infinite host, nor less for that
The flaming Seraph fearless, though alone   [875]
Encompassed round with foes, thus answered bold.
       O alienate from God, O Spirit accursed,
Forsaken of all good; I see thy fall
Determined, and thy hapless crew involved
In this perfidious fraud, contagion spread   [880]
Both of thy crime and punishment: henceforth
No more be troubled how to quit the yoke
Of God's Messiah; those indulgent laws
Will not be now vouchsafed, other decrees
Against thee are gone forth without recall;   [885]
That golden sceptre which thou didst reject
Is now an iron rod to bruise and break
Thy disobedience. Well thou didst advise,
Yet not for thy advice or threats I fly
These wicked tents devoted, lest the wrath   [890]
Impendent, raging into sudden flame
Distinguish not: for soon expect to feel
His thunder on thy head, devouring fire.
Then who created thee lamenting learn,
When who can uncreate thee thou shalt know.   [895]
       So spake the Seraph Abdiel faithful found,
Among the faithless, faithful only he;

Among innumerable false, unmoved,
Unshaken, unseduced, unterrified,
His loyalty he kept, his love, his zeal; [900]
Nor number, nor example with him wrought
To swerve from truth, or change his constant mind
Though single. From amidst them forth he passed,
Long way through hostile scorn, which he sustained
Superior, nor of violence feared aught; [905]
And with retorted scorn his back he turned
On those proud tow'rs to swift destruction doomed.

3. Book VI. 296–385

Raphael's account of the angelic war in heaven in Books V–VI has traditionally been regarded as one of the poem's weakest parts. Many readers and critics have registered their unhappiness with the portrayal of immortal angels squaring off in grand epic battle. Samuel Johnson sparked off the debate in its present form when he commented, 'The confusion of spirit and matter which pervades the whole narration of the war of heaven fills it with incongruity; and the book in which it is related is, I believe, the favourite of children, and gradually neglected as knowledge is increased'.[6] Johnson's assessment still rings true today, as the war in heaven chiefly narrated in Book VI is indeed one of the most neglected sequences in the poem. In creating the angelic war, Milton drew on similar depiction of warfare in classical epic, especially Homer's *Iliad* which also contains a rather comical sequence in which the immortal gods, who cannot really suffer serious wounds or die in combat, fight amongst themselves. In the *Iliad*, however, the aim is to contrast the frivolity of heavenly warfare and the Olympian gods more generally with the grim pathos and tragedy of heroic warfare among mortals. In Milton's heaven there is no such mirroring; the angelic war stands alone and if it is comical in places Milton wants that comedy to be at expense of the rebel angels themselves, who are ridiculous enough to wage war on an omnipotent God in the first place. The mockery and derision directed towards the rebel angels is best captured when God the Father himself, in an unsettling moment of crude anthropopathy, feigns panic and says to the Son, 'it now concerns us to be sure / Of our omnipotence ... Let us advise ... lest unawares we lose / This our high place, our sanctuary, our hill' (V. 721–32). God, of course, cannot be unaware of anything, nor need assurances of his omnipotence, but it does seem as if Milton has to have God play along with unfolding (and foreknown) events in order to make an example of the rebel angels. As Abdiel later reminds Satan, God 'with solitary hand / Reaching beyond all limit, at one blow / Unaided could have finished' (VI. 139–41) the rebels, but has chosen instead to let their war play out so that the other obedient angels and finally the Son as Messiah might get a chance to humble and punish their rebellious brothers in God's name.

The ensuing depiction of the war is in fact one of the more daring poetic sequences in the poem, rich with detail and striking images. Of course, as Johnson drily commented, many of the details in this wildly imaginative account of angelic warfare do not add up logically. Milton was evidently aware of the potential criticism and so brought to bear on the sequence his animist-materialist argument in elaborate asides which purport to explain angelic physiology. A typical example is when the narrator anxiously explains how beings of pure spirit may 'limb themselves, and colour, shape or size / Assume, as likes them best, condense or rare' (VI. 352–3), but nevertheless bleed 'nectarous humour' (VI. 332), feel pain and suffer 'ghastly wounds' (VI. 368). Once again we find ourselves in a Miltonic riddle which calls on us to filter a prelapsarian perspective through a postlapsarian one. The war in heaven is not allegorical, but neither is it strictly speaking literal. At the outset, Raphael concedes that although the monistic imperative of one continuous matter binds heaven and earth in closer proximity than is often supposed, the distances are nevertheless vast, requiring him as narrator to describe 'what surmounts the reach of human sense' by 'lik'ning spiritual to corporal forms, / As may express them best' (V. 573–4). However, as we have seen with the allegories of Sin and Death in the previous section, spiritual and corporal forms in Milton's universe are not merely relative terms. Such relativism in hell as well as in heaven repeatedly concedes the presence of fallen metaphor in the poem at large. The resulting spectacle may be implausible, and indeed as Raphael says 'unspeakable' (VI. 297), but as a literary creation aimed to teach a moral lesson about the price of disobedience it works poetic wonders. In the passage reproduced below, Raphael recounts how at the climax of the first phase of the war Satan and the archangel Michael squared off in single combat, like two mighty Homeric champions. He then proceeds to relate how the rest of the obedient angels then routed the rebels, whose angelic names have been blotted from heaven and are already replaced in Raphael's account proleptically with their demonic appellations.

> They ended parle, and both addresst for fight
> Unspeakable; for who, though with the tongue

Of angels, can relate, or to what things
Liken on earth conspicuous, that may lift
Human imagination to such heighth   [300]
Of godlike power: for likest gods they seemed,
Stood they or moved, in stature, motion, arms
Fit to decide the Empire of great Heav'n.
Now waved their fiery swords, and in the air
Made horrid circles; two broad suns their shields   [305]
Blazed opposite, while Expectation stood
In horror; from each hand with speed retired
Where erst was thickest fight, th' angelic throng,
And left large field, unsafe within the wind
Of such commotion, such as to set forth   [310]
Great things by small, if Nature's concord broke,
Among the constellations war were sprung,
Two planets rushing from aspéct malign
Of fiercest opposition in mid sky,
Should combat, and their jarring spheres confound.   [315]
Together both with next to Almighty arm,
Uplifted imminent one stroke they aimed
That might determine, and not need repeat,
As not of power, at once; nor odds appeared
In might or swift prevention; but the sword   [320]
Of Michael from the armoury of God
Was giv'n him tempered so, that neither keen
Nor solid might resist that edge: it met
The sword of Satan with steep force to smite
Descending, and in half cut sheer, nor stayed,   [325]
But with swift wheel reverse, deep ent'ring shared
All his right side; then Satan first knew pain,
And writhed him to and fro convolved; so sore
The griding sword with discontinuous wound
Passed through him, but th' ethereal substance closed   [330]
Not long divisible, and from the gash
A stream of nectarous humour issuing flowed
Sanguine, such as celestial Spirits may bleed,
And all his armour stained erewhile so bright.
Forthwith on all sides to his aid was run   [335]
By angels many and strong, who interposed
Defence, while others bore him on their shields
Back to his chariot, where it stood retired
From off the files of war; there they him laid
Gnashing for anguish and despite and shame   [340]
To find himself not matchless, and his pride

Humbled by such rebuke, so far beneath
His confidence to equal God in power.
Yet soon he healed; for Spirits that live throughout
Vital in every part, not as frail man   [345]
In entrails, heart or head, liver or reins,
Cannot but by annihilating die;
Nor in their liquid texture mortal wound
Receive, no more then can the fluid air:
All heart they live, all head, all eye, all ear,   [350]
All intellect, all sense, and as they please,
They limb themselves, and colour, shape or size
Assume, as likes them best, condense or rare.
    Meanwhile in other parts like deeds deserved
Memorial, where the might of Gabriel fought,   [355]
And with fierce ensigns pierced the deep array
Of Moloch furious king, who him defied,
And at his chariot wheels to drag him bound
Threatened, nor from the Holy One of Heav'n
Refrained his tongue blasphémous; but anon   [360]
Down cloven to the waist, with shattered arms
And uncouth pain fled bellowing. On each wing
Uriel and Raphaël his vaunting foe,
Though huge, and in a rock of diamond armed,
Vanquished Adramelech, and Asmadai,   [365]
Two potent Thrones, that to be less than gods
Disdained, but meaner thoughts learned in their flight,
Mangled with ghastly wounds through plate and mail.
Nor stood unmindful Abdiel to annoy
The atheist crew, but with redoubled blow   [370]
Ariel and Arioch, and the violence
Of Ramiel scorched and blasted overthrew.
I might relate of thousands, and their names
Eternize here on earth; but those elect
Angels contented with their fame in Heav'n   [375]
Seek not the praise of men: the other sort
In might though wondrous and in acts of war,
Nor of renown less eager, yet by doom
Cancelled from Heav'n and sacred memory,
Nameless in dark oblivion let them dwell.   [380]
For strength from Truth divided and from Just,
Illaudable, naught merits but dispraise
And ignominy, yet to glory aspires
Vainglorious, and through infamy seeks fame:
Therefore eternal silence be their doom.   [385]

4. Book X. 34–228

After the Fall, the Father sends the Son to pass judgement on Adam and Eve. The judgement scene, reproduced below from the opening of Book X, begins with another heavenly council between the Father and Son, mirroring in content almost exactly the council prior to the Fall in Book III. After reassuring the angels charged with guarding the gates of paradise that nothing they could have done would have prevented Satan's foreknown triumph, God again restates the central idea that no decree of his 'Concurr[ed] to necessitate [man's] Fall, / Or touch[ed] with lightest moment of impúlse / His free will' (X. 44–6), while the Son restates his wish to assume his interceding office of love and mercy and disclaims, 'Whoever judged, the worst on me must light' (X. 73). This close repetition of words and ideas spoken in Book III is meant not just to drive home the central message about free will, but also to lend support literarily to the eternal fixity of God's foreknowledge – the same ideas are expressed both before and after the fact indicating that God's eternal decree of free will is not itself affected by causality. The Son, now called God, assumes his Father's office and descends into the garden where he passes judgement on the serpent, on Satan *in absentia*, on Eve, and finally on Adam. This passage is interesting not just for its dramatisation of a human–divine exchange after the Fall, but also for its very close rewriting and expansion of Genesis 3: 8–21. It reveals much about Milton's engagement with his biblical source, where echoes of key verses interact with Miltonic asides and embellishments to create a wider and deeper dramatic effect within the original mythological constraints of the Bible. Milton's innovations here include the identification of the Genesis God with the Son, the turning of Genesis 3: 15 into a typological foreshadowing of the Son's final victory over Satan, and the very Protestant reference to Adam and Eve's 'much more / Opprobrious' inward nakedness which the Son proceeds to clothe 'with his robe of righteousness' (X. 221–2). There is also in this passage the charming narrator's aside in which the ever rationalist Milton registers his unhappiness with the logical non sequitur of the serpent's punishment (X. 164–70). In the original account in Genesis there is of course no mention of Satan. The idea that Satan possessed the serpent is a later Christian development, derived from the Apocrypha, later esoteric rabbinical teachings and Gnostic influences (see 'concepts and themes' in the commentary section below). This view has always posed a difficulty for Christian theologians reading Genesis in light of this tradition, because if the serpent was only possessed by Satan and is not itself the tempter, it has to be explained why God only punishes in the Genesis text the instrument and not the agent. Numerous theories have been proposed to explain this quirky exegetical anomaly. Milton, evidently worrying about this, follows a common exegetical tradition which argued that the serpent was justly punished by association. As the instrument of sin the serpent has been corrupted, or vitiated, by Satan, and is therefore, as the narrator notes, 'justly then accursed, / As vitiated in nature'. Milton, however, is still unsure and nevertheless adds in a rather anxious tone, 'more to know / Concerned not man (since he no further knew) / Nor altered his offence' (X. 168–71). Such asides remind us that Milton too is only human after all, and that even when the narrator presumes to speak for God in the poem and present images of heaven, the most that he can do is work with materials he gleans from scripture, imaginatively reworked to create the fiction of a lost knowledge fallen man could now never again presume to know.

> Assembled angels, and ye Powers returned
> From unsuccessful charge, be not dismayed,   [35]
> Nor troubled at these tidings from the earth,
> Which your sincerest care could not prevent,
> Foretold so lately what would come to pass,
> When first this Tempter crossed the gulf from Hell.
> I told ye then he should prevail and speed   [40]
> On his bad errand, man should be seduced
> And flattered out of all, believing lies
> Against his Maker; no decree of mine
> Concurring to necessitate his Fall,
> Or touch with lightest moment of impúlse   [45]
> His free will, to her own inclining left
> In even scale. But fall'n he is, and now
> What rests but that the mortal sentence pass
> On his transgression, death denounced that day,
> Which he presumes already vain and void,   [50]
> Because not yet inflicted, as he feared,
> By some immediate stroke; but soon shall find
> Forbearance no acquittance ere day end.
> Justice shall not return as bounty scorned.
> But whom send I to judge them? whom but thee   [55]
> Vicegerent Son, to thee I have transferred
> All judgment, whether in Heav'n, or earth, or Hell.
> Easy it might be seen that I intend
> Mercy colléague with justice, sending thee
> Man's friend, his Mediator, his designed   [60]
> Both ransom and Redeemer voluntary,

And destined man himself to judge man fall'n.
    So spake the Father, and unfolding bright
Toward the right hand his glory, on the Son
Blazed forth unclouded deity; he full   [65]
Resplendent all his Father manifest
Expressed, and thus divinely answered mild.
    Father Eternal, thine is to decree,
Mine both in Heav'n and earth to do thy will
Supreme, that thou in me thy Son beloved   [70]
May'st ever rest well pleased. I go to judge
On earth these thy transgressors, but thou know'st,
Whoever judged, the worst on me must light,
When time shall be, for so I undertook
Before thee; and not repenting, this obtain   [75]
Of right, that I may mitigate their doom
On me derived; yet I shall temper so
Justice with mercy, as may illústrate most
Them fully satisfied, and thee appease.
Attendance none shall need, nor train, where none   [80]
Are to behold the judgment, but the judged,
Those two; the third best absent is condemned,
Convíct by flight, and rebel to all law;
Conviction to the serpent none belongs.
    Thus saying, from his radiant seat he rose   [85]
Of high collateral glory: him Thrones and Powers,
Princedoms, and Dominations ministrant
Accompanied to Heaven gate, from whence
Eden and all the coast in prospect lay.
Down he descended straight; the speed of Gods   [90]
Time counts not, though with swiftest minutes winged.
Now was the sun in western cadence low
From noon, and gentle airs due at their hour
To fan the earth now waked, and usher in
The ev'ning cool when he from wrath more cool   [95]
Came the mild Judge and Intercessor both
To sentence man: the voice of God they heard
Now walking in the garden, by soft winds
Brought to their ears, while day declined; they heard
And from his presence hid themselves among   [100]
The thickest trees, both man and wife, till God
Approaching, thus to Adam called aloud.
    Where art thou Adam, wont with joy to meet
My coming seen far off? I miss thee here,
Not pleased, thus entertained with solitude,   [105]

Where obvious duty erewhile appeared unsought:
Or come I less conspicuous, or what change
Absents thee, or what chance detains? Come forth.
He came, and with him Eve, more loath, though first
To offend, discount'nanced both, and discomposed;   [110]
Love was not in their looks, either to God
Or to each other, but apparent guilt,
And shame, and perturbation, and despair,
Anger, and obstinacy, and hate, and guile.
Whence Adam falt'ring long, thus answered brief.   [115]
     I heard thee in the garden, and of thy voice
Afraid, being naked, hid myself. To whom
The gracious Judge without revile replied.
     My voice thou oft hast heard, and hast not feared,
But still rejoiced, how is it now become   [120]
So dreadful to thee? that thou art naked, who
Hath told thee? hast thou eaten of the tree
Whereof I gave thee charge thou shouldst not eat?
     To whom thus Adam sore beset replied.
O Heav'n! in evil strait this day I stand   [125]
Before my Judge, either to undergo
Myself the total crime, or to accuse
My other self, the partner of my life;
Whose failing, while her faith to me remains,
I should conceal, and not expose to blame   [130]
By my complaint; but strict necessity
Subdues me, and calamitous constraint,
Lest on my head both sin and punishment,
However insupportable, be all
Devolved; though should I hold my peace, yet thou   [135]
Wouldst easily detect what I conceal.
This woman whom thou mad'st to be my help,
And gav'st me as thy perfect gift, so good,
So fit, so ácceptáble, so divine,
That from her hand I could suspect no ill,   [140]
And what she did, whatever in itself,
Her doing seemed to justify the deed;
She gave me of the tree, and I did eat.
     To whom the sov'reign Presence thus replied.
Was she thy God, that her thou didst obey   [145]
Before his voice, or was she made thy guide,
Superior, or but equal, that to her
Thou didst resign thy manhood, and the place
Wherein God set thee above her made of thee,

And for thee, whose perfection far excelled   [150]
Hers in all real dignity: adorned
She was indeed, and lovely to attract
Thy love, not thy subjection, and her gifts
Were such as under government well seemed,
Unseemly to bear rule, which was thy part   [155]
And person, hadst thou known thyself aright.
    So having said, he thus to Eve in few:
Say woman, what is this which thou hast done?
    To whom sad Eve with shame nigh overwhelmed,
Confessing soon, yet not before her Judge   [160]
Bold or loquacious, thus abashed replied.
The serpent me beguiled and I did eat.
    Which when the Lord God heard, without delay
To judgement he proceeded on th' accused
Serpent though brute, unable to transfer   [165]
The guilt on him who made him instrument
Of mischief, and polluted from the end
Of his creation; justly then accursed,
As vitiated in nature: more to know
Concerned not man (since he no further knew)   [170]
Nor altered his offence; yet God at last
To Satan first in sin his doom applied,
Though in mysterious terms, judged as then best:
And on the serpent thus his curse let fall.
    Because thou hadst done this, thou art accursed   [175]
Above all cattle, each beast of the field;
Upon thy belly grovelling thou shalt go,
And dust shalt eat all the days of thy life.
Between thee and the woman I will put
Enmity, and between thine and her seed;   [180]
Her seed shall bruise thy head, thou bruise his heel.
    So spake this oracle, then verified
When Jesus son of Mary second Eve,
Saw Satan fall like lightning down from Heav'n,
Prince of the Air; then rising from his grave   [185]
Spoiled Principalities and Powers, triúmphed
In open show, and with ascension bright
Captivity led captive through the air,
The realm itself of Satan long usurped,
Whom he shall tread at last under our feet;   [190]
Ev'n he who now foretold his fatal bruise,
And to the woman thus his sentence turned.
    Thy sorrow I will greatly multiply

By thy conception; children thou shalt bring
In sorrow forth, and to thy husband's will   [195]
Thine shall submit, he over thee shall rule.
        On Adam last thus judgement he pronounced.
Because thou hast hearkened to the voice of thy wife,
And eaten of the tree concerning which
I charged thee, saying: Thou shalt not eat thereof,   [200]
Cursed is the ground for thy sake, thou in sorrow
Shalt eat thereof all the days of thy life;
Thorns also and thistles it shall bring thee forth
Unbid, and thou shalt eat the herb of the field,
In the sweat of thy face shalt thou eat bread,   [205]
Till thou return unto the ground, for thou
Out of the ground wast taken; know thy birth,
For dust thou art, and shalt to dust return.
        So judged he man, both Judge and Saviour sent,
And th' instant stroke of death denounced that day   [210]
Removed far off; then pitying how they stood
Before him naked to the air, that now
Must suffer change, disdained not to begin
Thenceforth the form of servant to assume,
As when he washed his servants' feet, so now   [215]
As father of his family he clad
Their nakedness with skins of beasts, or slain,
Or as the snake with youthful coat repaid;
And thought not much to clothe his enemies:
Nor he their outward only with the skins   [220]
Of beasts, but inward nakedness, much more
Opprobrious, with his robe of righteousness,
Arraying covered from his Father's sight.
To him with swift ascent he up returned,
Into his blissful bosom reassumed   [225]
In glory as of old, to him appeased,
All, though all-knowing, what had passed with man
Recounted, mixing intercession sweet.

Commentary and analysis

Concepts and themes

In the opening invocation to the poem the poet pleads of the 'Heav'nly Muse' (I. 6) to instruct and illumine him 'That to the heighth of this great argument / I may assert Eternal Providence, / And justify the ways of God to men' (I. 24–6). As noted in Chapter 1, the project of theodicy in *Paradise Lost* is a highly audacious, not to say heretical enterprise, born in large part from Milton's idiosyncratic belief in the need for individual Christians to be held both morally and *rationally* accountable before God. The audacity of the verbs 'assert' and 'justify', however, is meant to establish Milton's prophetic authority over the fallen reader, not over God. Although a 'satanic' reading of the poem might conclude that Milton puts God on trial, what is in fact on trial throughout the poem is the reader's culpability and ongoing complicity in the Fall. *Paradise Lost* never presumes as a poem to justify, in the sense of 'apologising for', God's more abstract and unknowable will, but it does seek to indict fallen man's disobedience before God which led to man's just loss of paradise to begin with. The argument set out in God's speeches, especially during the council in heaven between the Father and the Son in Book III (passage 1 above), is therefore a carefully thought-out sermon on Milton's, not God's, theology. To point this out is not to be cynical. The Father's theology, after all, represents a set of ideas which Milton firmly believed were entirely consonant with a rational interpretation of Scripture and therefore with God's will. However, in making a claim for the logic of this theology Milton invites logical scrutiny of that theology and so risks in places undermining the entire project of theodicy. I say 'risks', because despite all the logical flaws and contradictions in the argument, Milton also goes out of his way to sustain the argument affectively and poetically, and whether he succeeds or not remains a question each individual reader needs to answer for themselves.

From a conceptual point of view, the most important idea to take from the Father's speech in Book III is that free will, decreed to man as a divine gift of reason, has shaped the human experience from its inception, and defines our failings and hopes as God's creatures. The Father sets out his vision of divine justice in the heavenly council in two stages. The first stage makes the case for the decree of free will while the second stage, reacting to the Son's searching questions about mercy, deals with the decrees of election and grace after the Fall. In the first stage of the argument, the decree of free will depends logically on the important anti-Calvinist qualification that for God to foreknow is never to foreordain. Here, however, the urge to argue yields its first quibble. No matter how strongly Milton insists that when it comes to God foreknowing does not necessitate foreordaining, it is a distinction which is impossible to sustain from the position of 'fallen' logical causality without at some stage straining the credibility of God's omnipotence. Calvin knew as much, and Milton like the Arminians before him has to live with the resulting paradox of denying this. This difficulty is reflected for example in Milton's use of the word 'shall' in III. 92, when God states that Satan 'shall' pervert man. It has been suggested that the sudden shift between tenses in the Father's speech is meant to capture the idea that a foreknowing God is above time, but our minds do not work that way. To most readers 'shall' rings too much like the pronouncement of an irrevocable decree of the same God who declares elsewhere in the poem, 'what I will is Fate' (VII. 173). Despite these difficulties, however, Milton insists in the poem on the distinction between foreknowing and foreordaining and pushes it to potentially heretical extremes. When the Father next defensively concedes that even if he had not foreknown, the Fall still would have happened, God's omnipotence is utterly shattered:

> they themselves decreed
> Their own revolt, not I: if I foreknew,
> Foreknowledge had no influence on their fault,
> Which had no less proved certain unforeknown.
> (III. 116–19)

Milton is forced logically to back-peddle here into truly alien theological territory. If in fact, as indirectly implied here, the Fall was a predetermined event entirely beyond God's control, then the thought creeps in not only that God is not omnipotent, but that there must be other forces of causality at work in the pre-created universe which are, potentially, even more powerful than God. It is doubtful whether this idea, bordering on the edge of extreme Gnostic dualism, was something Milton intentionally aiming for, but it nevertheless hovers on the edge of his theology as a heretical possibility.

According to the ancient Gnostic heresy there are not one, but two Gods. There is the truly transcendental good God, who is detached from creation, and then there is the evil maker God, the demiurge, who created this world and man within it. In the Gnostic heresy, it was Christ, not Satan, who, disguised as the serpent of Genesis, offered humanity wisdom and thereby redemption from the evil of created flesh. In eating of the Tree of Knowledge and knowing good and evil humanity was given the key to ascend back to the absolute goodness of the transcendental God through a process of inner knowledge, or 'gnosis'. This heresy, despite being thrust to the margins of Christian thought in the early stages of the Church's history, nevertheless continued to haunt orthodox Christian theology throughout its development and it haunts Milton's theodicy and strident monism in *Paradise Lost* as well.[7] It casts a long shadow of doubt on the anti-Trinitarian subordination of the Son to a potentially 'unjust' Father and animates much of Satan's counter-messianic narrative. It also strains the theology of free will in the poem. The Father created man 'just and right, / Sufficient to have stood, though free to fall', but he must have done so while at least foreknowing that man *will* Fall. Given that God foreknows all, what does it mean then in this context to create man 'sufficient to have stood'? Sufficiency implies that God endowed man with rational faculties and therefore created him a priori sufficient in the sense of 'capable' to withstand any temptation (OED adj. 3a, *obs*, citing this line as an example). However, 'sufficient' also implies in the more usual sense of the adjective (OED adj. 1a) that prior to the Fall the Father will also provide man only with the sufficient *amount* and *kind* of knowledge *necessary* to stand. This is certainly the rationale behind Raphael's instructive mission to Adam and Eve later in the poem in rendering them 'inexcusable'. However, from our fallen perspective it seems that no prior knowledge, short of exactly the forbidden knowledge of good and evil, could have adequately prevented the Fall, and so enters the distinctly Gnostic heretical thought that Satan, disguised as the serpent, was actually seeking to liberate Adam and Eve from the tyranny of an evil God. Moreover, the further question rises that if God foreknew that man would fall in an absolute sense, what was the point of the exercise in creating man 'sufficient' to begin with, unless the aim all along (as Empson suspected) was for God simply to acquit himself in Milton's poem from the responsibility for evil in the world. In fact, absurdly we have to confront the uncomfortable idea that in foreknowing the Fall, God deliberately must have created man *insufficient* so as not to contradict his own foreknowledge.

These paradoxes and potential heresies have beset the myth of the Fall in Judaeo-Christian theology from its inception, and Milton should not be taken to task as a poet for not being able to do anything about them. Arguably, Milton is merely exploiting an inherent logical contradiction within the received mythology in an effort once again to confront his readers with complex interpretative choices. In this regard, it is possible and indeed desirable to point out that the difference between foreknowledge and foreordination in the Father's speech in Book III and in the poem at large is less an abstract metaphysical quibble and more of a moral imperative: Milton does not want us to judge God's will through fallen human standards, but to grasp the central point that man should never use the excuse of predestination to abdicate moral responsibility. As the Father says,

Not free, what proof could they have giv'n sincere
Of true allegiance, constant faith or love,

Where only what they needs must do, appeared,
Not what they would? What praise could they receive?
(III. 103–6)

Free will is never an antonym to obedience in *Paradise Lost*, but absolutely depends on it. The line between responsible moral agency and
licentious anarchy is a fine one, but it is perhaps the most important
ethical distinction the reader is required to make throughout the poem.
God endowed humanity with free will so God might enjoy their freely
given obedience and worship, not that humans might do as they please
and consequently rebel. For Milton, fallen humanity is free therefore to
do only one thing essentially: freely to choose reason and the obedience to
God's will it dictates. As the Father declares in a poignant parenthetical
aside, 'reason also is choice' (III. 108). From this rational choice all true
moral freedom and liberty flows. In disobeying, in knowing for oneself
good and evil, man paradoxically forfeits his free will and becomes like
the devils 'enthralled' to sin. After the Fall, it is only through grace and
the intercession and sacrifice of the Son that regenerated humans have
some measure of 'free will' restored to them and may, through faith in
Christ, choose again to obey and so be liberated from sin.

As we move from the Father's discussion of foreknowledge and free
will to his doctrine of grace and election in the second stage of the
council with the Son, we begin to see therefore that Milton's quarrel
with Calvin is complex and never unequivocal. There is in this speech
a great deal of residual Calvinism in the celebration of the Father's
majesty and power, in the presentation of the Father's decree of free
will as binding rather than liberating, and, as noted above, in the several
apparent inconsistencies within the phrasing of the theology itself.
Dennis Danielson and more recently Stephen Fallon (see bibliography)
have both written cogently about the complex Calvinist resonance of
the Father's words when discussing, for example, the promise of saving
grace to the elect:

Some I have chosen of peculiar grace
Elect above the rest; so is my will:
The rest shall hear me call, and oft be warned
Their sinful state, and to appease betimes
Th' incensèd Deity, while offered grace
Invites; for I will clear their senses dark,
What may suffice, and soften stony hearts
To pray, repent, and bring obedience due.
(III. 183–90)

The idea expressed here is entirely consistent with an Arminian outlook of prevenient grace. God declares that his gift of grace is open also to those not numbered among the 'elect', who may in accepting grace pray, repent, and finally be saved in newfound obedience. Significantly, Milton does not brand the 'rest' as reprobates, or speak of their damnation as absolute. However, inexplicably from an Arminian point of view Milton does have God declare that 'some I have chosen of peculiar grace / Elect above the rest'. Who are these 'elect' and what is the meaning of their 'peculiar grace'? The attempt to distinguish between different types of grace was typical of developments within English Calvinism, where some thinkers tried to account for the various apparent dispositions of different people within the overall scheme of predestination. Several leading puritan divines, for example William Perkins and later Richard Baxter, grappled with the question as to why some sinners who are manifest reprobates in their behaviour nevertheless do good in some cases. Since free will was out of the question, it was proposed that God must endow even reprobates with some measure of 'sufficient' or 'temporary' grace, not that they might save themselves, but that they might confirm the elect in their state of 'efficient' grace by doing good works. Milton's 'peculiar grace', however, is neither 'sufficient' nor 'efficient'. It implies in fact a sense of unique privilege, as if to suggest that notwithstanding the decree of free will and saving grace to all, God nevertheless predestined a select few for unconditional salvation, among whom Milton presumably numbered himself (otherwise why even mention this?). The difference between Milton's 'peculiar grace' and similar definitions in contemporary Calvinist theology is stark. For Calvinists, the 'elect' are simply a small group of abject sinners whom God chose to save in his impenetrable will and mercy. The theology which emerges from the Father's speech in the passage above, however, strongly implies that those endowed with 'peculiar grace' are precisely *not* sinners, since they do not need to pray and repent like the 'rest' of fallen humanity, and this is consistent with Milton's sense of himself as somehow sinless. As Stephen Fallon has shown, this surprising concession to Calvinist predestination is not meant to contradict the fundamentally Arminian tenor of the Father's speech, but is emblematic of Milton's irreconcilable desire to be both predestined for greatness and virtuously worthy of such election.[8]

Style and form
The conceptual integrity of what the Father and the Son say in their respective dialogues and speeches may come under logical scrutiny and

even appear flawed in places, but the affective and dramatic impact of *what* they say largely depends in the poem on stylistic effects within the speeches themselves and the imagery framing them. However, if the content of the heavenly council has engaged some critics in a scholarly argument over its theological interpretation, the argument over the style and tone of divine speech in *Paradise Lost* has proved radically divisive. The problem with God's style is that it appeals both to logic and emotion in equal measure and the two traditionally do not sit well together. On one side, then, there are those critics who emphasise the rational aspects of divine speech in the poem as the most salient, and who then seek to rationalise or dismiss any apparent display of emotion as subordinate to the logic being expressed. On the other side there are those critics who insist that the emotional and dramatic aspects of divine speech in the poem are the most important in rendering as persuasive an otherwise logically flawed theology. The rationalists usually dismiss out of hand the emotional argument, while the emotionalists accept the rational argument but seek to qualify it.

It is undeniable that cold rationality is a central stylistic effect of divine speech in the poem. If Satan's rhetoric works on principles of misdirection and relies on convoluted, self-contradictory syntax, the Father's style is characterised by short, carefully balanced sentences complemented by the use of logical antithesis and symmetry rather than the more contradictory chiastic structures we encounter in Satan's speeches. Significantly, Milton's God also avoids conditional clauses and tends in his expression towards abstract nouns which suggest something of his eternity and infinity. The problem, however, is that this stylistic design is undermined when Milton also employs the device of anthropopathy and ascribes to God powerful human-like emotion. One of the most controversial cruxes in this respect is the Father's use of the word 'ingrate' in his apparently emotional reaction to his own foreknowledge about the Fall:

> so will fall
> He and his faithless progeny: whose fault?
> Whose but his own? Ingrate, he had of me
> All he could have; I made him just and right,
> Sufficient to have stood, though free to fall.
> (III. 95–9)

The word 'ingrate' strikes such a petulant chord in our ears that the tightly condensed theological dogma so crucial to the poem's project of justification contained in 'I made him just and right, / Sufficient to have stood, though free to fall' is hard, if not impossible, for some readers to digest. Matters are not made any easier when we also reflect (reluctantly perhaps) that in the earlier treatise of *De Doctrina* Milton directly rejects the use of anthropopathy in theological discourse as a 'rhetorical device thought up by grammarians to explain the nonsense poets write about Jove', and, moreover, that it is 'better not to think about God or form an image of him in anthropopathetic terms, for to do so would be to follow the example of men, who are always inventing more and more subtle theories about him'.[9]

There are several ways to approach this problem. One way is of course to dismiss *De Doctrina* as irrelevant to *Paradise Lost* by insisting that the two texts have very little in common either generically or substantially, and what is true of one need not be true of the other. However, it is also possible to argue that the two texts actually agree with each other on this point by qualifying in different ways the definition of anthropopathy and anthropomorphism more generally in Milton's portrayal of God in the poem. According to a rationalist reading, for example, the modern reader tends to over-complicate the problem by placing too much emphasis on his or her own unsolicited emotional response to divine speech. God is not being defensive or petulant but merely logical, and a word such as 'ingrate', as Fish for example argues, is 'a term not of reproach, but of definition'.[10] Alternatively, it is possible to qualify Milton's use of anthropopathy not by appealing to logic but by referring to the literary convention of the Bible. After all, the tone of righteous indignation Milton attributes to his speaking God is entirely commensurate with similar biblical passages where God expresses dismay or frustration with his creatures. Such is the tone, as Milton himself points out in *De Doctrina*, in Genesis 6: 6, or indeed in Numbers 14: 11: 'And the Lord said unto Moses, How long will this people provoke me? and how long will it be ere they believe me, for all the signs which I have shewed them?' Milton could be said therefore to be judiciously biblical in his use of anthropopathy and this would suit well with his comment in *De Doctrina* that 'we should form our ideas [about God] with scripture as a model, for that is the way in which he has offered himself to our contemplation'.[11] Finally, however, these qualifications may be labouring the point too strongly. It is not inconceivable that an unsolicited emotional response from the reader is precisely what Milton was aiming for in *Paradise Lost*. The debate between the Father and the Son is meant not just to explain things, but also to arouse powerful emotions of shame and guilt in the reader which place the cold meditation on the doctrinal pronouncements in their proper spiritual context. When the Father lashes out with the word 'ingrate', it is Milton the poet after all, not God, who is registering his disgust with fallen humanity.

Moreover, divine speech in *Paradise Lost* is always reported within the didactic epic frame of the inspired poet's narrative, and its cumulative effect must be weighed against the imaginary backdrop of the poem as a whole. Therefore, given the sensitivity of these passages when God speaks, it is important to pay attention not just to the content of the speeches, but also to the imagery used to frame and introduce the divine speakers, for example in Book III with a description of God the Father on his throne (passage 1 above):

> Now had th' Almighty Father from above,
> From the pure Empyrean where he sits
> High throned above all heighth, bent down his eye,
> His own works and their works at once to view:
> About him all the sanctities of Heaven
> Stood thick as stars, and from his sight received
> Beatitude past utterance
> (III. 56–62)

The significance of this description, which insists on the unsayable and unknowable remoteness of God's unmediated presence, *is* that it conforms to traditional descriptions of the hidden God in Christian mysticism and liturgy. The traditional anthropomorphic references to God 'sitting' and 'bending his eye' are balanced by the idea that God sits, transcendentally, 'above all heighth' and that the beatitude he bestows on the angels is 'past utterance'. Moreover, once God's speech is concluded, the narrator hastens to add:

> Thus while God spake, ambrosial fragrance filled
> All Heav'n, and in the blessèd Spirits elect
> Sense of new joy ineffable diffused
> (III. 135–7)

This extraordinary olfactory image, suggesting that God's words fill heaven with 'ambrosial fragrance', colours the speech which we have just read with a profound sense of otherworldly mystery that ingeniously proceeds from the inherent anthropomorphism of the imagery. The anthropomorphic God who sits and talks also produces sweet breath *as* he talks. But this anthropomorphic breath does not behave as normal breath does – God, we are reminded, is not a man – for as the breath spreads throughout all heaven its 'ambrosial fragrance' causes a new sense of ineffable 'joy' to spread among the angels who smell it. By the force of the same trope, God's otherwise literal words are not merely heard in heaven, but are in fact felt as a total sensory and emotional experience. By framing God's literal speech with a sense of profound mystery, Milton reminds us that what we read when God speaks and must understand literally is in fact radically unsayable at its source. This move instantly creates a split in the representation of God in the poem, since it points out that were God the Father to speak directly to the reader the experience would overwhelm us. Moreover, it attaches the deep emotion and fear usually associated with the mystery of God's unmediated presence to the literalness of his words, so that what God says carries with it throughout the epic a deep, resounding authority.

Historical-political context

The first time we encounter overt political ideas and language in the poem we find that we are in the presence of devils. The modern reader is perhaps happy to discover that political ideas and forms of discourse in *Paradise Lost* thrive in hell. After all, there is something undeniably infernal about the perceived dishonesty, relativism and pragmatism of politicians pretending to lofty ideals about truth and liberty, but who only promote their self-interest. We expect therefore Satan to be a politician playing fast and loose with such terms as 'liberty' and 'tyranny', but we are surprised when we discover in the poem that obedient, unfallen angels and even God are strangely political beings. Like hell, Milton's heaven is also portrayed as a grand political establishment, with a monarch, assemblies, ranks of angels performing 'ministeries due and solemn rites' (VII. 149), a standing army, and even an 'armoury' (VI. 321). The parallels with hell are of course deliberate. Milton wants us to note the glaring similarities between the councils in hell and heaven and worry about them, but then also to work out the important differences. Once discerned, these subtle differences in the political language applied in each case, often bordering on nuance, slowly map out the available alternatives laid before Milton's 'fit' readers: just as there is a fallen form of political governance and debate, there is also a pre-fallen heavenly model based on right reason and the rigid paradox of hierarchal equality under God's unassailable sovereignty as Creator. What drive this debate within the poem are the all important ideas of true as opposed to false liberty and the role of 'right reason' as an arbiter. The archangel Michael alludes to these differences directly when he instructs the fallen Adam about what was lost after the Fall, and what this now means for the pursuit of liberty in a fallen world:

Since thy original lapse, true liberty
Is lost, which always with right reason dwells
Twinned, and from her hath no dividual being:
Reason in man obscured, or not obeyed,
Immediately inordinate desires
And upstart passions catch the government
From reason, and to servitude reduce
Man till then free. Therefore since he permits
Within himself unworthy powers to reign
Over free reason, God in judgement just
Subjects him from without to violent lords;
Who oft as undeservedly enthrall
His outward freedom: tyranny must be,
Though to the tyrant thereby no excuse,
Yet sometimes nations will decline so low
From virtue, which is reason, that no wrong
But justice, and some fatal curse annexed
Deprives them of their outward liberty,
Their inward lost
(XII. 83–101)

The key idea here and throughout the poem is that outward liberty in the state proceeds from inner liberty of conscience, freely exercised by the individual creature rationally choosing to obey God's will implicit in the 'Concord and law of nature' (XII. 28). The unfallen angels, therefore, like man before the Fall, enjoy in heaven 'fair equality' and 'fraternal state' (XII. 25), even though they are not all equal in rank before God 'In their triple degrees' (V. 749–50), while fallen beings, even though apparently equal in rank or state, are no better than slaves if they have abdicated their 'right reason'.

The aim then of the overt politicisation and even militarisation of heaven in *Paradise Lost* is not to produce a political allegory as such, but to allow us to see God's monarchy in action using terms of reference from the fallen world we might recognise. Raphael's account of the verbal confrontation between Satan and Abdiel in Book V (passage 2 above) captures in miniature the tension which results from this close similarity between heavenly and fallen perspectives on political ideas. However, it is not a simple case of Satan being flatly wrong because he is a compulsive liar and of Abdiel in this case being flatly right because he is an obedient angel. Raphael may preface the account by pointing out that Satan held his audience of rebel angels 'with calumnious art / Of counterfeited truth' (V. 770–1), but it is Satan, not Abdiel, who appeals first to cogent principles of liberty one would expect a republican like

Milton to endorse. Amid his torrent of lies and equivocations, Satan nevertheless voices the central tenet of Milton's belief in hierarchal monism, where 'orders and degrees / Jar not with liberty, but well consist':

> Will ye submit your necks, and choose to bend
> The supple knee? ye will not, if I trust
> To know ye right, or if ye know yourselves
> Natives and sons of Heav'n possessed before
> By none, and if not equal all, yet free,
> Equally free; for orders and degrees
> Jar not with liberty, but well consist.
> Who can in reason then or right assume
> Monarchy over such as live by right
> His equals, if in power and splendour less,
> In freedom equal?
> (V. 787–97)

Instead of having Abdiel pronounce unchallenged this important idea about equality within hierarchy, Milton significantly first shows Satan slyly subverting the implications of this idea in seeking to elide God's rightful monarchy as creator with the assumed monarchy of an arbitrary tyrant. In denying God's rightful pre-eminence as Creator Satan can then easily claim that the angels before the promotion of the Son were 'possessed ... By none', and that, moreover, degrees in heaven are merely superficial since 'by right' all angels are equals of God. It is only after Satan is shown misrepresenting this important idea that Milton then has Abdiel correct this error, not, however, by restating the same idea from a position of obedience, but by affirming the duty of the servant in a language which to fallen ears sounds very close to the royalist rhetoric of absolutism:

> Canst thou with impious obloquy condemn
> The just decree of God, pronounced and sworn,
> That to his only Son by right endued
> With regal sceptre, every soul in Heav'n
> Shall bend the knee, and in that honour due
> Confess him rightful King? unjust thou say'st
> Flatly unjust, to bind with laws the free,
> And equal over equals to let reign,
> One over all with unsucceeded power.
> (V. 813–21)

This careful inversion of political ideas in heaven and the blurring of fallen political discourse of resistance and obedience implies that the right and wrong of any political action – be it rebellion or obsequious knee-bending – depends on the context in which it is performed and on the ability of the individual conscience to discern the differences in any given case. In heaven, as Abdiel points out, to rebel against God's decrees is paradoxically to 'bind with laws the free', not to free those bound by any law. Milton's antinomianism shines through here very brightly: God's monarchy is not based on any law or outer compulsion, but on angels willingly and rationally worshipping God in harmonious order and degree which flows from the inside out as a matter of individual choice. Milton's angels choose to obey because they *know* as a matter of inner discernment it is the right thing to do, not because they have been persuaded or otherwise compelled; the rebel angels on the other hand have to be persuaded and compelled by Satan to betray this initial choice.

As a narrative distinction between heaven and hell the above inversions are clear enough, but the reader's true burden of interpretation is to work out how to apply these distinctions in the troubled politics of the fallen world. The politics of the poem may be remote to us today, but this was not meant to be an easy task of interpretation even for Milton's 'fit' intended readers. Milton projects onto the pre- and post-lapsarian divide of the poem contemporary debates about sovereignty and the role of the political executive to secure liberty for its people, but these ideas are abstract in the extreme. *Paradise Lost* is not an essay in political theory; it does not promote a republican constitutional arrangement over a monarchical one, and cannot be enlisted (despite numerous attempts to do so by readers then as now) to endorse this or that political agenda absolutely, only a certain political attitude. Satan, Abdiel, Michael and Adam all fall back on republican language at moments in the poem in an effort to articulate their respective understanding of what it means to enjoy true liberty. However, the main idea for the reader to grasp from this polyphony of voices speaking in similar terms is that politics for Milton is not a matter of stating facts, but of debating them. If angels can debate the finer points of politics in heaven, then the need for such debate after the Fall, when truth must battle it out openly with falsehood, is absolutely imperative. Satan's open challenge to God's monarchy in heaven forces the reader to assess and dispute the principles of true liberty not as stated facts but as contested ideas. Politicians today often talk about bringing back integrity and transparency to political culture, and if this sounds implausible it is because most people, even the most idealistic, do not associate integrity and transparency with political processes. Most people, however, can still appreciate the value of free

and informed debate as a remedy against the corruption and atrophy
of politics, and Milton is still one of our most vocal and challenging
teachers in this lost art.

Paradise, Adam and Eve, and the Fall

Paradise Lost is an epic poem about epic loss. As we have seen already
with the settings of hell and heaven, the loss is spiritual, occasionally
political and always universal. However, as we set our eyes on the main
stage of paradise and of the human couple at its centre we realise that
what is finally at stake is the deeply personal loss of humanity's innocence, and of obedient and truly harmonious filial as well as conjugal
love. The settings of hell and heaven function as epic digressions of
immense scope which frame the smaller setting of paradise at the poem's
tragic core. By comparison, paradise is a very intimate domestic space,
which like the great households of Greek and Shakespearean tragedy
contains the seeds of great calamity in its fragile state of harmony. It is
often remarked that Milton portrays paradise as a strangely fallen place,
where Adam and Eve, as one critic famously put it, behave in all respects
like two 'suburbanites in the nude'.[12] There is indeed an undeniably
bourgeois quality to Adam and Eve's prelapsarian, idealised domesticity;
they potter in the garden, have guests for tea and go through the motions
of sober conjugal sex. The domestic familiarity of Adam and Eve's life
before the Fall is not an anomaly but an integral part of Milton's design
which views marriage as a prelapsarian institution established by God in
Genesis 2: 18 and 2: 23–4 along the ideals of intellectual companionship
and friendship between the first man and woman. Unlike Satan or God,
Adam and Eve are meant to be close to us, not just as archetypes but as
Milton's utopian models for future living in the fallen world. Satan may
seem frighteningly human in places and God perplexingly so, but Adam
and Eve *are* humans, and all that separates them from us before the Fall
are shades of innocence and untried obedience. Milton constantly wants
us to hold onto the idea that the trials of the prelapsarian past are the
trials of the lapsarian future and that paradise is not therefore irrevocably lost. As the Father remarks foreknowingly, fallen humanity may
eventually 'by degrees of merit raised . . . open to themselves at length
the way / Up hither, under long obedience tried, / And earth be changed
to Heav'n' (VII. 157–60).

In hell and heaven the differences between merely human 'fallen'
perspectives and imagined 'pre-fallen' ones are vast, but in paradise
they are painfully small. Indeed, the finer the distinctions between

pre- and postlapsarian love, sexuality and conjugal bliss in Milton's paradise, the greater our sense as readers of the impending tragedy and the loss it incurs. Innocence in Milton's paradise is not, therefore, a simple romantic notion about innate goodness and blissful ignorance, but is synonymous with the same ideas of liberty, obedience and right reason foregrounding the bigger, universal story of Satan's rebellion and the Father's proclamation of his foreknown justice. Adam and Eve before the Fall embody the ideals of 'true filial freedom' (IV. 294) in the human domestic sphere, where there is nevertheless clear subordination between husband and wife. As the now infamous line declares, 'He for God only, she for God in him' (IV. 299). These much maligned words, implying Eve's complete subjection to Adam before God, point, however, to a complex and often inconsistent ideal of qualified human freedom within unequal relationships which is absolutely central to the poem's project of theodicy. Many readers rightly object today to the patriarchal, condescending manner in which Milton presents in the poem the ideal relationship between the sexes, but the implied patriarchal hierarchy extends far beyond crude misogyny. Like it or not, the idea that Adam and Eve are unified before God only as long as the rational Adam rules over the more sensual Eve is crucial to the idea of the Fall in the poem and to its overarching lesson about the loss of freedom that comes with the abdication of right reason. Although not absolving Eve of her culpability, her rational subordination in effect places the responsibility for the Fall squarely on Adam who should have known better. Moreover, the moment in the poem when Adam chooses to fall for love rather than remain forever alone is perhaps one of the most startling implications Milton draws from this patriarchal paradigm. Adam may be superior to Eve, but he cannot live without her. Herein lies one of Milton's most provocative ideas in the poem, that what defines us as created human beings is our necessarily asymmetrical relationships with each other. As Adam says to God, 'In solitude / What happiness, who can enjoy alone, / Or all enjoying, what contentment find?' (VIII. 364–6). Only the infinite and eternal God who is above creation can exist alone in a truly self-sufficient manner. Singularity in God implies perfection, but in the creature of God it implies, as Adam realises, a state of 'single imperfection . . . In unity defective, which requires / Collateral love, and dearest amity' (VIII. 423–6). Adam and Eve are plainly 'Not equal, as their sex not equal seemed' (IV. 296), and their inequality, despite what this line suggests, is not merely physical. But in their prelapsarian state they also represent a model of a 'happy nuptial league' (IV. 339), where man and wife enjoy an absolutely *equal* measure of companionship based on 'collateral love'. In this respect Eve is not merely subordinate to Adam, she completes him in a profound existential and theological sense. Whether or not Adam also completes Eve or actually interferes with her autonomy is a different question altogether, but it is a question Milton shies away from, except when he allows Eve to toy with its possibilities once she eats of the forbidden fruit.

Eve may be subordinate to Adam theologically, but from a literary point of view Eve is arguably more interesting than Adam as a character. Adam is presented as mild-mannered, inquisitive and precociously bright, but he is also quite one-dimensional. Eve, on the other hand, is necessarily complex. Even before the Fall Eve dreams, doubts, and resists, and, once tempted by Satan, even contemplates other possible lives. Milton's Eve has indeed attracted much critical attention in her own right over the decades, especially from critics who detect in her quietly subversive manner of 'sweet reluctant amorous delay' (IV. 310) an early modern proto-feminist narrative running against the grain of the poem's overt patriarchal assumptions. Although it is unlikely that Milton can be seriously praised today as a proto-feminist, it is undeniable that his Eve is a far cry from the vain temptress of traditional biblical exegesis and art. Although Milton stuck to the frame of the Genesis story in making Eve both the victim and the unwitting agent of temptation, he nevertheless created in her a multilayered mythic character that, much like Satan, draws us in and beguiles by suggesting to us narratives and ideas which run counter to the main argument put forward by the poem's narrator and other voices of authority. However, where Satan is seductive in a dangerous, defiant manner, Eve is more allusive and intriguing in a subtle way. Milton constantly frames Eve with deeply suggestive mythic allusions and images which point to her ambivalent role as the disobedient, narcissistic agent of the Fall but also as the chaste, fertile matriarch of mankind whom Milton hails without a hint of malice 'our mother Eve' (XII. 624). Similarly to Satan, therefore, Eve is also a protean figure who undergoes considerable change in the poem, but unlike Satan her progression moves from juvenile self-love and error into maternal maturity and meekness. Eve's striking sensuality throughout this process, like that of the garden she so lovingly tends, is a function of her ever changing literary and mythic resonance. Much more than Adam, it is Eve who embodies in this way the aesthetics and ethics of a lost paradise. Her beauty and flawed character, but also her deep intelligence, remind us that what lost us paradise in a moment's error, and what equally might finally regain us such bliss through long trial of obedience, is our irredeemable humanity on our mother's side. After all, the last lines of Milton's later brief epic of *Paradise Regained* end with Jesus, having withstood Satan's temptations, returning 'unobserved / Home to his mother's house' (IV. 638–9).

Key passages

1. Book IV. 205–355

The first time in the poem we are shown a vista of paradise before the Fall we see it through Satan's eyes (the 'him' of line 205), and we see it as he does with an acute sense of loss. The passage below, describing the delights of the garden and introducing us for the first time to Adam and Eve in their Edenic bliss, is couched between Satan's despairing monologues as he reacts to this sight (see passages 3 and 4 in the 'hell' section above). In his reimagining of paradise Milton relies on several devices which point to its fundamental absence from our fallen existence. Complex negative similes and elaborate mythological allusions to fabulous gardens containing hidden danger complement an artificial vision of opulence, where streams issuing from a 'sapphire fount' roll 'on orient pearl and sands of gold' (IV.237–8), and where 'fruit burnished with golden rind' hang 'amiable' (IV. 249–50). Milton goes on to say of the golden fruit of paradise that they are 'Hesperian fables true, / If true, here only, and of delicious taste' (IV. 250–1). Such imagery, alluding to the mythic garden of the Hesperides (which also contained a tree bearing golden fruit of immortality), suggests a wondrous mythology or fable wrought by the poet's artful fancy that 'if true', so the poet muses, it can only be so 'here', in paradise. But of course paradise is *not* to be found 'here', in the poem, since it is in fact already lost. It is into this decidedly fictional setting that Milton then allows Adam and Eve to emerge into view for the first time 'with native honour clad / In naked majesty' (IV. 289–90). The sense of loss already attending the baroque reimagining of the Garden of Eden frames the human couple inhabiting it so that we recognise their humanity only in remote emblematic and moral terms. Adam's 'eye sublime' for example 'declare[s] / Absolute rule' (IV. 300–1), while his 'manly' forelock of shoulder-length hair anticipates the Pauline link between hairstyles and the hierarchy of the sexes in 1 Cor. 11: 1–15. In line with this scriptural tradition, Eve's 'unadornèd golden tresses' wave about in 'wanton ringlets', suggesting a degree of unruly sexuality but also coy 'Subjection' (IV. 308) and a natural chasteness. Eve's hair is perhaps one of the most charged images in this passage. The wanton waves of her tresses, curling emblematically as the 'vine' (IV. 307), point to her fertility and nuptial subordination to Adam, but also insinuate hidden serpentine danger. To seal this association, Milton next echoes Eve's hair imagery in the description of the 'serpent sly' lying ominously close by, 'Insinuating, wove with Gordian twine / His braided train' (IV. 347–9). The phrase 'braided train' contrasts with the idea that Eve's prelapsarian beauty consists of specifically 'unadorned' hair, and is therefore as yet blameless of the sinfulness prefigured proleptically in the serpent's 'Insinuating' presence. Milton thus knits Eve and the serpent together in this passage through distinctly 'fallen' metaphors deriving from art and craft rather than the natural world (note for example later in Book IX. 525 the reference to the serpent's 'enamelled neck'). The passage contrasts in this way the profuseness of 'Nature boon' (IV. 242) in paradise with the limits of a 'nice art' (IV. 241), pointing out obliquely that what man had before the Fall naturally he can only recreate and approximate after the Fall artificially. This passage is therefore crucial for the poem as a whole because it decidedly brackets Milton's art of poetry with all flawed human endeavour potentially tainted by sin.

Beneath him with new wonder now he views	[205]
To all delight of human sense exposed	
In narrow room Nature's whole wealth, yea more,	
A Heav'n on earth, for blissful Paradise	
Of God the garden was, by him in the east	
Of Eden planted; Eden stretched her line	[210]
From Auran eastward to the royal towers	
Of great Seleucia, built by Grecian kings,	
Or where the sons of Eden long before	
Dwelt in Telassar: in this pleasant soil	
His far more pleasant garden God ordained;	[215]
Out of the fertile ground he caused to grow	
All trees of noblest kind for sight, smell, taste;	
And all amid them stood the Tree of Life,	
High eminent, blooming ambrosial fruit	
Of vegetable gold; and next to life	[220]
Our death the Tree of Knowledge grew fast by,	
Knowledge of Good bought dear by knowing ill.	
Southward through Eden went a river large,	
Nor changed his course, but through the shaggy hill	
Passed underneath ingulfed, for God had thrown	[225]
That mountain as his garden mould high raised	
Upon the rapid current, which through veins	
Of porous earth with kindly thirst up drawn,	
Rose a fresh fountain, and with many a rill	
Watered the garden; thence united fell	[230]

Down the steep glade, and met the nether flood,
Which from his darksome passage now appears,
And now divided into four main streams,
Runs diverse, wand'ring many a famous realm
And country whereof here needs no account,   [235]
But rather to tell how, if art could tell,
How from that sapphire fount the crispèd brooks,
Rolling on orient pearl and sands of gold,
With mazy error under pendent shades
Ran nectar, visiting each plant, and fed   [240]
Flow'rs worthy of Paradise which not nice art
In beds and curious knots, but Nature boon
Poured forth profuse on hill and dale and plain,
Both where the morning sun first warmly smote
The open field, and where the unpierced shade   [245]
Embrowned the noontide bowers: thus was this place,
A happy rural seat of various view;
Groves whose rich trees wept odorous gums and balm,
Others whose fruit burnished with golden rind
Hung amiable, Hesperian fables true,   [250]
If true, here only, and of delicious taste:
Betwixt them lawns, or level downs, and flocks
Grazing the tender herb, were interposed,
Or palmy hillock, or the flow'ry lap
Of some irriguous valley spread her store,   [255]
Flow'rs of all hue, and without thorn the rose:
Another side, umbrageous grots and caves
Of cool recess, o'er which the mantling vine
Lays forth her purple grape, and gently creeps
Luxuriant; meanwhile murmuring waters fall   [260]
Down the slope hills, dispersed, or in a lake,
That to the fringèd bank with myrtle crowned,
Her crystal mirror holds, unite their streams.
The birds their choir apply; airs, vernal airs,
Breathing the smell of field and grove, attune   [265]
The trembling leaves, while universal Pan
Knit with the Graces and the Hours in dance
Led on th' eternal spring. Not that fair field
Of Enna, where Prosérpine gath'ring flow'rs
Herself a fairer flow'r by gloomy Dis   [270]
Was gathered, which cost Ceres all that pain
To seek her through the world; nor that sweet grove
Of Daphne by Orontes, and th' inspired
Castalian spring, might with this Paradise

Of Eden strive; nor that Nyseian isle   [275]
Girt with the river Triton, where old Cham,
Whom Gentiles Ammon call and Libyan Jove,
Hid Amalthea and her florid son
Young Bacchus from his stepdame Rhea's eye;
Nor where Abássin kings their issue guard,   [280]
Mount Amara, though this by some supposed
True Paradise under the Ethiop line
By Nilus' head, enclosed with shining rock,
A whole day's journey high, but wide remote
From this Assyrian garden, where the Fiend   [285]
Saw undelighted all delight, all kind
Of living creatures new to sight and strange:
Two of far nobler shape erect and tall,
Godlike erect, with native honour clad
In naked majesty seemed lords of all,   [290]
And worthy seemed, for in their looks divine
The image of their glorious Maker shone,
Truth, wisdom, sanctitude severe and pure,
Severe, but in true filial freedom placed;
Whence true authority in men; though both   [295]
Not equal, as their sex not equal seemed;
For contemplation he and valour formed,
For softness she and sweet attractive grace,
He for God only, she for God in him:
His fair large front and eye sublime declared   [300]
Absolute rule; and hyacinthine locks
Round from his parted forelock manly hung
Clust'ring, but not beneath his shoulders broad:
She as a veil down to the slender waist
Her unadornèd golden tresses wore   [305]
Dishevelled, but in wanton ringlets waved
As the vine curls her tendrils, which implied
Subjection, but required with gentle sway,
And by her yielded, by him best received,
Yielded with coy submission, modest pride,
And sweet reluctant amorous delay.   [310]
Nor those mysterious parts were then concealed;
Then was not guilty shame, dishonest shame
Of nature's works, honour dishonourable,
Sin-bred, how have ye troubled all mankind   [315]
With shows instead, mere shows of seeming pure,
And banished from man's life his happiest life,
Simplicity and spotless innocence.

So passed they naked on, nor shunned the sight
Of God or angel, for they thought no ill: [320]
So hand in hand they passed, the loveliest pair
That ever since in love's embraces met,
Adam the goodliest man of men since born
His sons, the fairest of her daughters Eve.
Under a tuft of shade that on a green   [325]
Stood whispering soft, by a fresh fountain side
They sat them down, and after no more toil
Of their sweet gard'ning labour than sufficed
To recommend cool Zephyr, and made ease
More easy, wholesome thirst and appetite   [330]
More grateful, to their supper fruits they fell,
Nectarine fruits which the compliant boughs
Yielded them, sidelong as they sat recline
On the soft downy bank damasked with flow'rs:
The savoury pulp they chew, and in the rind   [335]
Still as they thirsted scoop the brimming stream;
Nor gentle purpose, nor endearing smiles
Wanted, nor youthful dalliance as beseems
Fair couple, linked in happy nuptial league,
Alone as they. About them frisking played   [340]
All beasts of th' earth, since wild, and of all chase
In wood or wilderness, forest or den;
Sporting the lion ramped, and in his paw
Dandled the kid; bears, tigers, ounces, pards
Gambolled before them, th' unwieldy elephant   [345]
To make them mirth used all his might, and wreathed
His lithe proboscis; close the serpent sly
Insinuating, wove with Gordian twine
His braided train, and of his fatal guile
Gave proof unheeded; others on the grass   [350]
Couched, and now filled with pasture gazing sat,
Or bedward ruminating: for the sun
Declined was hasting now with prone career
To th' Ocean Isles, and in th' ascending Scale
Of Heav'n the stars that usher evening rose: [355]

2. Book IV. 440–91; Book VIII. 249–578

The Book of Genesis contains two separate and seemingly contradictory accounts of humanity's creation. Genesis 1: 27 simply states that
on the sixth day of creation God 'created man in his *own* image, in the
image of God created he him; male and female created he them'. Then,

however, in Genesis 2: 7–25, a much more detailed account introduces the more familiar myth in which God first created Adam and placed him the garden, and only then created 'woman' from Adam's rib 'and brought her unto the man' (2: 22). The Adam and Eve we encounter in their emblematic bliss in Book IV (passage 1 above) are very much the human couple of Genesis 1: 27, male and female, placed in the garden as lords over God's creation, but with Eve taking a clearly subordinate role, as she does not have direct access to God and was not formed in his presumably masculine image (as strongly implied in Genesis 1: 27). As Adam and Eve begin to converse later in the book, Milton reinforces these distinctions as he moves to the second, more complex narrative of creation, but here Milton suddenly veers dramatically from any orthodox interpretation of the Genesis myth. Seizing on the literary and narrative potential offered by the gaps in the Genesis account of Eve's creation from Adam's rib, Milton startles the reader by having Eve, not Adam, recount her moment of creation as *she* remembers it. Then later in Book VIII, Milton does the same for Adam who recounts to the angel Raphael what he remembers of his first waking thoughts and feelings after being created by God. The two creation narratives as remembered and retold by Eve and Adam retrospectively (reproduced below together) have been much debated by critics of the poem. While superficially the obvious differences between the two narratives reinforce Eve's subordination to Adam (Eve looks down, Adam looks up, Eve has to be coerced into submission, Adam exercises intuitive knowledge), crucial similarities between them complicate this view in allowing us to think of Adam and especially of Eve as autonomous human beings struggling to form their distinct sense of self within an imposed theological paradigm.

Eve's awakening memory has attracted by far the most attention simply by virtue of being so unique. Milton has Eve recount to Adam how she first awoke by the side of a pool and instantly fell in love with her own reflection before being coerced by the voice of God to leave the pool and join Adam in the garden. Milton creatively alludes here to Ovid's account from *Metamorphoses*, iii. 339–510, of the myth of Narcissus – the beautiful youth who wasted away and was metamorphosed into a flower after obsessing lovingly over his own reflection in a pool. There are many possible ways of interpreting Eve's awakening scene in light of this allusion, but one obvious reading is to see in it an embedded lesson on the threat of idolatry that comes from self-love and self-reliance. As we noted with Satan, reflexivity is the mark of the idolater in *Paradise Lost*; in pining towards her own reflected beauty,

Eve runs the risk of wasting away in idolatry. Crucially, however, Eve does so with 'unexperienced thought' (IV. 457). Her striking beauty carries with it the *potential* for sin, but she herself is innocent of its seductive entanglements and is saved from herself by God's patriarchal voice of reason which leads her away from the pool to Adam's side (echoing in fact the words of Ovid's narrator pleading with Narcissus to turn away from his reflection). However, rather than immediately submitting to Adam, Eve's initial instinct is to resist her subordinate status as if to imply that there is something decidedly unnatural about the patriarchal paradigm being imposed on her. Even in obedient hindsight she recalls, perhaps fondly, perhaps bitterly, that she initially found Adam's appearance 'Less winning soft, less amiably mild, / Than that smooth wat'ry image' (IV. 479–80) and so turned to flee, forcing Adam to grab her by the hand and violently assert his authority. Eve eventually concedes that 'beauty is excelled by manly grace / And wisdom' (IV. 489–90), but her account raises more questions than it answers, especially about the exact nature of human createdness before the Fall. God evidently created Eve beautiful, but we begin to sense that he also deliberately created Eve *seductively* beautiful to test both her and Adam. The impact of Eve's beauty is indeed at the heart of Adam's memory of the same event recounted later in Book VIII. When Adam sees Eve for the first time, even though he is not yet fallen, he is overawed by her beauty and reason deserts him. As if suspecting that this might prove a potential problem in the very near future, Adam shares with the angel truly heretical thoughts. Not wanting to blame God for his inability to stay composed before Eve's 'loveliness', he blames 'Nature' instead for bestowing on Eve 'Too much of ornament, in outward show / Elaborate, of inward less exact' (VIII. 538–9), and goes on to protest that 'All higher knowledge in her presence falls / Degraded, wisdom in discourse with her / Looses discount'nanced and like folly shows' (VIII. 551–3). Adam's words, as one would expect, meet a swift rebuke from the angel through whose admonishing, 'with contracted brow' (VIII. 560), Milton once again delivers a sermon on the threat of enjoying sexual intercourse for its own sake, on the merit of intellectual love and companionship between married couples, and the central refrain that the gift of free will must be managed by the judicious use of right reason given especially to the man as a mark of his superiority over woman. It also sets up the scene for the ensuing drama of the Fall, conditioning us to accept the novel idea that Adam is far more culpable than Eve for bearing the greater share of responsibility for their joint obedience.

Book IV. 440–91

    To whom thus Eve replied. O thou for whom   [440]
And from whom I was formed flesh of thy flesh,
And without whom am to no end, my guide
And head, what thou hast said is just and right.
For we to him indeed all praises owe,
And daily thanks, I chiefly who enjoy   [445]
So far the happier lot, enjoying thee
Pre-eminent by so much odds, while thou
Like consort to thyself canst nowhere find.
That day I oft remember, when from sleep
I first awaked, and found myself reposed   [450]
Under a shade of flow'rs, much wond'ring where
And what I was, whence thither brought, and how.
Not distant far from thence a murmuring sound
Of waters issued from a cave and spread
Into a liquid plain, then stood unmoved   [455]
Pure as th' expanse of heav'n; I thither went
With unexperienced thought, and laid me down
On the green bank, to look into the clear
Smooth lake, that to me seemed another sky.
As I bent down to look, just opposite,   [460]
A shape within the wat'ry gleam appeared
Bending to look on me: I started back,
It started back, but pleased I soon returned,
Pleased it returned as soon with answering looks
Of sympathy and love; there I had fixed   [465]
Mine eyes till now, and pined with vain desire,
Had not a voice thus warned me, What thou seest,
What there thou seest fair creature is thyself,
With thee it came and goes: but follow me,
And I will bring thee where no shadow stays   [470]
Thy coming, and thy soft embraces, he
Whose image thou art, him thou shall enjoy
Inseparably thine, to him shalt bear
Multitudes like thyself, and thence be called
Mother of human race: what could I do,   [475]
But follow straight, invisibly thus led?
Till I espied thee, fair indeed and tall,
Under a platan, yet methought less fair,
Less winning soft, less amiably mild,
Than that smooth wat'ry image; back I turned,   [480]
Thou following cried'st aloud, Return, fair Eve;
Whom fli'st thou? Whom thy fli'st, of him thou art,

His flesh, his bone; to give thee being I lent
Out of my side to thee, nearest my heart
Substantial life, to have thee by my side   [485]
Henceforth an individual solace dear;
Part of my soul I seek thee, and thee claim
My other half: with that thy gentle hand
Seized mine, I yielded, and from that time see
How beauty is excelled by manly grace   [490]
And wisdom, which alone is truly fair.

Book VIII. 249–578
    So spake the Godlike Power, and thus our sire.
For man to tell how human life began   [250]
Is hard; for who himself beginning knew?
Desire with thee still longer to converse
Induced me. As new waked from soundest sleep
Soft on the flow'ry herb I found me laid
In balmy sweat, which with his beams the sun   [255]
Soon dried, and on the reeking moisture fed.
Straight toward heav'n my wond'ring eyes I turned,
And gazed a while the ample sky, till raised
By quick instinctive motion up I sprung,
As thitherward endeavouring, and upright   [260]
Stood on my feet; about me round I saw
Hill, dale, and shady woods, and sunny plains,
And liquid lapse of murmuring streams; by these,
Creatures that lived, and moved, and walked, or flew,
Birds on the branches warbling; all things smiled,   [265]
With fragrance and with joy my heart o'erflowed.
Myself I then perused, and limb by limb
Surveyed, and sometimes went, and sometimes ran
With supple joints, as lively vigour led:
But who I was, or where, or from what cause,   [270]
Knew not; to speak I tried, and forthwith spake,
My tongue obeyed and readily could name
Whate'er I saw. Thou sun, said I, fair light,
And thou enlightened earth, so fresh and gay,
Ye hills and dales, ye rivers, woods, and plains,   [275]
And ye that live and move, fair creatures, tell,
Tell, if ye saw, how came I thus, how here?
Not of myself; by some great Maker then,
In goodness and in power pre-eminent;
Tell me, how may I know him, how adore,   [280]
From whom I have that thus I move and live,

And feel that I am happier than I know.
While thus I called, and strayed I knew not whither,
From where I first drew air, and first beheld
This happy light, when answer none returned,   [285]
On a green shady bank profuse of flow'rs
Pensive I sat me down; there gentle sleep
First found me, and with soft oppression seized
My drowsèd sense, untroubled, though I thought
I then was passing to my former state   [290]
Insensible, and forthwith to dissolve:
When suddenly stood at my head a dream,
Whose inward apparition gently moved
My fancy to believe I yet had being,
And lived: one came, methought, of shape divine,   [295]
And said, thy mansion wants thee, Adam, rise,
First man, of men innumerable ordained
First father, called by thee I come thy guide
To the garden of bliss, thy seat prepared.
So saying, by the hand he took me raised,   [300]
And over fields and waters, as in air
Smooth sliding without step, last led me up
A woody mountain; whose high top was plain,
A circuit wide, enclosed, with goodliest trees
Planted, with walks, and bowers, that what I saw   [305]
Of earth before scarce pleasant seemed. Each tree
Loaden with fairest fruit that hung to the eye
Tempting, stirred in me sudden appetite
To pluck and eat; whereat I waked, and found
Before mine eyes all real, as the dream   [310]
Had lively shadowed: here had new begun
My wand'ring, had not he who was my guide
Up hither, from among the trees appeared,
Presence divine. Rejoicing, but with awe
In adoration at his feet I fell   [315]
Submiss: he reared me, and Whom thou sought'st I am,
Said mildly, Author of all this thou seest
Above, or round about thee or beneath.
This Paradise I give thee, count it thine
To till and keep, and of the fruit to eat: [320]
Of every tree that in the garden grows
Eat freely with glad heart; fear here no dearth:
But of the tree whose operation brings
Knowledge of good and ill, which I have set
The pledge of thy obedience and thy faith,   [325]

Amid the garden by the Tree of Life,
Remember what I warn thee, shun to taste,
And shun the bitter consequence: for know,
The day thou eat'st thereof, my sole command
Transgressed, inevitably thou shalt die;   [330]
From that day mortal, and this happy state
Shalt lose, expelled from hence into a world
Of woe and sorrow. Sternly he pronounced
The rigid interdiction, which resounds
Yet dreadful in mine ear, though in my choice   [335]
Not to incur; but soon his clear aspéct
Returned and gracious purpose thus renewed.
Not only these fair bounds, but all the earth
To thee and to thy race I give; as lords
Possess it, and all things that therein live,   [340]
Or live in sea, or air, beast, fish, and fowl.
In sign whereof each bird and beast behold
After their kinds; I bring them to receive
From thee their names, and pay thee fealty
With low subjection; understand the same   [345]
Of fish within their wat'ry residence,
Not hither summoned, since they cannot change
Their element to draw the thinner air.
As thus he spake, each bird and beast behold
Approaching two and two, these cow'ring low   [350]
With blandishment, each bird stooped on his wing.
I named them, as they passed, and understood
Their nature, with such knowledge God endued
My sudden apprehension: but in these
I found not what methought I wanted still;   [355]
And to the Heav'nly vision thus presumed.
        O by what name, for thou above all these,
Above mankind, or aught than mankind higher,
Surpassest far my naming, how may I
Adore thee, Author of this universe,   [360]
And all this good to man, for whose well-being
So amply, and with hands so liberal
Thou hast provided all things: but with me
I see not who partakes. In solitude
What happiness, who can enjoy alone,   [365]
Or all enjoying, what contentment find?
Thus I presumptuous; and the vision bright,
As with a smile more brightened, thus replied.
        What call'st thou solitude, is not the earth

With various living creatures, and the air   [370]
Replenished, and all these at thy command
To come and play before thee? Know'st thou not
Their language and their ways? They also know,
And reason not contemptibly; with these
Find pastime, and bear rule; thy realm is large.   [375]
So spake the Universal Lord, and seemed
So ordering. I with leave of speech implored,
And humble deprecation thus replied.
      Let not my words offend thee, Heav'nly Power,
My Maker, be propitious while I speak.   [380]
Has thou not made me here thy substitute,
And these inferior far beneath me set?
Among unequals what society
Can sort, what harmony or true delight?
Which must be mutual, in proportion due   [385]
Giv'n and received; but in disparity
The one intense, the other still remiss
Cannot well suit with either, but soon prove
Tedious alike: of fellowship I speak
Such as I seek, fit to participate   [390]
All rational delight, wherein the brute
Cannot be human consort; they rejoice
Each with their kind, lion with lioness;
So fitly them in pairs thou hast combined;
Much less can bird with beast, or fish with fowl   [395]
So well converse, nor with the ox the ape;
Worse then can man with beast, and least of all.
      Whereto th' Almighty answered, not displeased.
A nice and subtle happiness I see
Thou to thyself proposest, in the choice   [400]
Of thy associates, Adam, and wilt taste
No pleasure, though in pleasure, solitary.
What think'st thou then of me, and this my state?
Seem I to thee sufficiently possessed
Of happiness, or not? who am alone   [405]
From all eternity, for none I know
Second to me or like, equal much less.
How have I then with whom to hold converse
Save with the creatures which I made, and those
To me inferior, infinite descents   [410]
Beneath what other creatures are to thee?
      He ceased, I lowly answered. To attain
The heighth and depth of thy eternal ways

All human thoughts come short, supreme of things;
Thou in thy self art perfect, and in thee   [415]
In no deficience found; not so is man,
But in degree, the cause of his desire
By conversation with his like to help,
Or solace his defects. No need that thou
Shouldst propagate, already infinite;   [420]
And through all numbers absolute though One;
But man by number is to manifest
His single imperfection, and beget
Like of his like, his image multiplied,
In unity defective, which requires   [425]
Collateral love, and dearest amity.
Thou in thy secrecy although alone,
Best with thyself accompanied, seek'st not
Social communication, yet so pleased,
Canst raise thy creature to what heighth thou wilt   [430]
Of union or communion, deified;
I by conversing cannot these erect
From prone, nor in their ways complacence find.
Thus I emboldened spake, and freedom used
Permissive, and acceptance found, which gained   [435]
This answer from the gracious voice divine.
　　　　Thus far to try thee, Adam, I was pleased,
And find thee knowing not of beasts alone,
Which thou hast rightly named, but of thyself,
Expressing well the spirit within thee free,   [440]
My image, not imparted to the brute,
Whose fellowship therefore unmeet for thee
Good reason was thou freely shouldst dislike,
And be so minded still; I, ere thou spak'st,
Knew it not good for man to be alone,   [445]
And no such company as then thou saw'st
Intended thee, for trial only brought,
To see how thou could'st judge of fit and meet:
What next I bring shall please thee, be assured,
Thy likeness, thy fit help, thy other self,   [450]
Thy wish exactly to thy heart's desire.
　　　　He ended, or I heard no more, for now
My earthly by his Heav'nly overpowered,
Which it had long stood under, strained to the heighth
In that celestial colloquy sublime,   [455]
As with an object that excels the sense,
Dazzled and spent, sunk down, and sought repair

Of sleep, which instantly fell on me, called
By nature as in aid, and closed mine eyes.
Mine eyes he closed, but open left the cell   [460]
Of Fancy my internal sight, by which
Abstráct as in trance methought I saw,
Though sleeping, where I lay, and saw the shape
Still glorious before whom awake I stood,
Who stooping opened my left side, and took   [465]
From thence a rib, with cordial spirits warm,
And life-blood streaming fresh; wide was the wound,
But suddenly with flesh filled up and healed:
The rib he formed and fashioned with his hands;
Under his forming hands a creature grew,   [470]
Manlike, but different sex, so lovely fair,
That what seemed fair in all the world, seemed now
Mean, or in her summed up, in her contained
And in her looks, which from that time infused
Sweetness into my heart, unfelt before,   [475]
And into all things from her air inspired
The spirit of love and amorous delight.
She disappeared, and left me dark, I waked
To find her, or forever to deplore
Her loss, and other pleasures all abjure: [480]
When out of hope, behold her, not far off,
Such as I saw her in my dream, adorned
With what all earth or Heaven could bestow
To make her amiable: on she came,
Led by her Heav'nly Maker, though unseen,   [485]
And guided by his voice, nor uninformed
Of nuptial sanctity and marriage rites:
Grace was in all her steps, Heav'n in her eye,
In every gesture dignity and love.
I overjoyed could not forbear aloud.   [490]
    This turn hath made amends; thou hast fulfilled
Thy words, Creator bounteous and benign,
Giver of all things fair, but fairest this
Of all thy gifts, nor enviest. I now see
Bone of my bone, flesh of my flesh, my self   [495]
Before me; woman is her name, of man
Extracted; for this cause he shall forgo
Father and mother, and to his wife adhere;
And they shall be one flesh, one heart, one soul.
    She heard me thus, and though divinely brought,   [500]
Yet innocence and virgin modesty,

Her virtue and the conscience of her worth,
That would be wooed, and not unsought be won,
Not obvious, not obtrusive, but retired,
The more desirable, or to say all,   [505]
Nature herself, though pure of sinful thought,
Wrought in her so, that seeing me, she turned;
I followed her, she what was honour knew,
And with obsequious majesty approved
My pleaded reason. To the nuptial bow'r   [510]
I led her blushing like the Morn: all Heav'n,
And happy constellations on that hour
Shed their selectest influence; the earth
Gave sign of gratulation, and each hill;
Joyous the birds; fresh gales and gentle airs   [515]
Whispered it to the woods, and from their wings
Flung rose, flung odours from the spicy shrub,
Disporting, till the amorous bird of night
Sung spousal, and bid haste the e'vning star
On his hill top, to light the bridal lamp.   [520]
Thus have I told thee all my state, and brought
My story to the sum of earthly bliss
Which I enjoy, and must confess to find
In all things else delight indeed, but such
As used or not, works in the mind no change,   [525]
Not vehement desire, these delicacies
I mean of taste, sight, smell, herbs, fruits and flow'rs,
Walks, and the melody of birds; but here
Far otherwise, transported I behold,
Transported touch; here passion first I felt,   [530]
Commotion strange, in all enjoyments else
Superior and unmoved, here only weak
Against the charm of beauty's powerful glance.
Or Nature failed in me, and left some part
Not proof enough such object to sustain,   [535]
Or from my side subducting, took perhaps
More than enough; at least on her bestowed
Too much of ornament, in outward show
Elaborate, of inward less exact.
For well I understand in the prime end   [540]
Of Nature her th' inferior, in the mind
And inward faculties, which most excel,
In outward also her resembling less
His image who made both, and less expressing
The character of that dominion giv'n   [545]

O'er other creatures; yet when I approach
Her loveliness, so absolute she seems
And in herself complete, so well to know
Her own, that what she wills to do or say,
Seems wisest, virtuousest, discreetest, best;   [550]
All higher knowledge in her presence falls
Degraded, wisdom in discourse with her
Looses discount'nanced and like folly shows;
Authority and reason on her wait,
As one intended first, not after made   [555]
Occasionally; and to consúmmate all,
Greatness of mind and nobleness their seat
Build in her loveliest, and create an awe
About her, as a guard angelic placed.
To whom the angel with contracted brow.   [560]
      Accuse not Nature, she hath done her part;
Do thou but thine, and be not diffident
Of Wisdom; she deserts thee not, if thou
Dismiss not her, when most thou need'st her nigh,
By áttribúting overmuch to things   [565]
Less excellent, as thou thyself perceiv'st.
For what admir'st thou, what transports thee so,
An outside? fair no doubt, and worthy well
Thy cherishing, thy honouring, and thy love,
Not thy subjection: weigh with her thyself;   [570]
Then value: oft times nothing profits more
Than self-esteem, grounded on just and right
Well managed; of that skill the more thou know'st,
The more she will acknowledge thee her head,
And to realities yield all her shows: [575]
Made so adorn for thy delight the more,
So awful, that with honour thou may'st love
Thy mate, who sees when thou art seen least wise.

3. Book IX. 192–411

The tragedy of the Fall in *Paradise Lost* unfolds over the course of Book
IX. Consequently, Book IX is one of the most dramatic in the poem, not
just in its overall pathos and the sense of impending doom attending its
narrative, but also in its theatrical structure, the pacing of its action and
dialogues, and the heavy use of dramatic perspectives, repetitions and
devastating tragic irony. The book consists of three parts, or scenes:
Adam and Eve's separation in the garden, Satan's temptation of Eve, and
Eve's temptation of Adam. The first of these, the so-called 'separation

scene', is reproduced here below. In the eyes of many critics and readers of the poem the moment when Adam reluctantly allows Eve to depart from him in the garden is in tragic terms the fatal error which leads to the inevitable catastrophe – it is to all intents and purposes what Aristotle defines in his *Poetics* as the tragic mistake, or *hamartia*, committed in ignorance or folly, after which there is no turning back for the tragic protagonists. The moment Eve softly withdraws her hand from Adam's (IX. 385–6) and departs to divide their labour in the garden is presented as a moment of decisive calamity. The didactic point is clear: Adam and Eve, each to themselves suffering from 'single imperfection', united stand but divided fall. The narrator draws attention to this moment, calling their separation an 'event perverse!' (IX. 405), as he heaps on the departing Eve a series of gloomy mythological allusions, likening her to Delia (Diana), Ceres, Pomona and Proserpina (Persephone). The epic simile attached to Eve at that moment is perhaps one of Milton's most complex and ambiguous in the poem. Milton associates her with a number of pagan goddesses traditionally identified with chastity, fertility and agricultural cultivation but then qualifies and obscures the details in such a way as to suggest that in the moments leading up to the Fall these same allusions can only evoke a sense of Eve's fickleness and sexual volatility, as well as the threat of rape and corruption which now ominously looms over her. The famous myth of Persephone's abduction by Pluto, god of the underworld, which resulted in the division of an otherwise eternal spring into four seasons and the birth of agriculture, is especially offered up here as a dark mythological backdrop. Satan's violation of Eve will similarly result in the end of Eden's vernal bliss and bring about after the Fall the toil and harsh conditions implicit in the seasonal cycles of the agricultural year.

Milton draws attention in this way to the tragic enormity of Eve's departure, but the dialogue which leads up to this rupture is anything but straightforward in terms of the didactic message it yields. From the point of view of the poem's theodicy and overarching argument about obedience and free will Eve is of course wrong in wanting to divide their labour in the garden, and Adam is right in initially resisting this. Eve's most glaring error is her misunderstanding of the concept of 'labour' in Eden. She suggests that they divide their gardening chores so they can achieve more in less time, as if she is already a fallen being chaffing under the burden of quotas. Adam is quick to point out that in their Edenic state pruning or loping in a garden 'tending to wild' (IX. 212) is not meant to be a chore, but a recreational 'delight' which (one assumes) would give them something to do as they share their time together – a way perhaps to assert their control over the garden, not to cultivate in any way a garden which requires no cultivation. Eve, however, does not respond well to her husband's superior reasoning and what ensues is the first lovers' quarrel (we must note with a growing sense of irony that, technically speaking, the Fall has not happened yet). Although she is innocent and has no notion of good or evil, Eve shows remarkable mental and rhetorical agility in raising a powerful objection to Adam's patriarchal rule: if they are meant always to be together out of necessity or threat rather than choice, 'Frail is our happiness, if this be so, / And Eden were no Eden thus exposed' (IX. 340–41). Adam's stern reply, 'best are all things as the will / Of God ordained them' (IX. 343–4) is reasoned and predictable, but strikingly evasive. Moreover, the irony produced by the echoing of previous phrases spoken by God and Raphael in different contexts unbalances the reader even further. Eve echoes, of all characters, God himself when she hurls at Adam the rhetorical question, 'And what is faith, love, virtue unassayed / Alone, without exterior help sustained?' (IX. 335–6), while Adam in turn echoes the words of Raphael, previously addressed to him as a rebuke, by telling Eve, 'God towards thee hath done his part, do thine' (IX. 375). These echoes do more than challenge the reader to make difficult discriminations; they also point to difficulties with the central argument about the nature of true liberty raised throughout the poem. Adam's decision to let Eve depart hinges on a crucial misunderstanding of free will as Milton presents it. Adam mistakenly thinks that if Eve is constrained to stay against her will he is somehow violating her freedom of choice gifted to her by God. The narrator makes it clear that in this respect Adam makes a fatal and tragic error: Adam lets Eve go when in fact he should have made her stay, by force if necessary, since that would have been the rational, obedient thing to do in the eyes of God. Eve simply lacks the rational clarity which Adam possesses and therefore should have been overruled like a child. However, consciously or otherwise, Milton allows the humanity of the scene to break through and flatten these abstract patriarchal ideas. The fallen reader, then as now, knows that on a deep human level Eve is absolutely right in her objection and that Adam is therefore equally right when he concedes movingly, 'for thy stay, not free, absents thee more' (IX. 372). Here we get a fuller sense of the impossible closeness between the pre- and postlapsarian perspectives where Adam and Eve are concerned. In reality no person, including Milton, can rightly envision humanity in a prelapsarian state without resorting to moral and theological platitudes. In venturing so far beyond the Genesis myth in an attempt to portray the inner life of the first human couple before the Fall,

Milton constantly found he was describing human beings as he knew them, not as theological concepts. The only way he could ever make the story of the Fall matter to his readers is by portraying Adam and Eve's trespass as a tragic error born of their *inherently* fallen humanity. In theology this amounts to an absurd heresy and in philosophy to an illogical contradiction, but in literature such a non sequitur translates into high drama and deeply engaging narrative poetry.

> Now when as sacred light began to dawn
> In Eden on the humid flow'rs, that breathed
> Their morning incense, when all things that breathe,
> From th' earth's great altar send up silent praise   [195]
> To the Creator, and his nostrils fill
> With grateful smell, forth came the human pair
> And joined their vocal worship to the choir
> Of creatures wanting voice; that done, partake
> The season, prime for sweetest scents and airs: [200]
> Then cómmune how that day they best may ply
> Their growing work: for much their work outgrew
> The hands' dispatch of two gard'ning so wide.
> And Eve first to her husband thus began.
>   Adam, well may we labour still to dress   [205]
> This garden, still to tend plant, herb and flow'r,
> Our pleasant task enjoined, but till more hands
> Aid us, the work under our labour grows,
> Luxurious by restraint; what we by day
> Lop overgrown, or prune, or prop, or bind,   [210]
> One night or two with wanton growth derides
> Tending to wild. Thou therefore now advise
> Or hear what to my mind first thoughts present;
> Let us divide our labours, thou where choice
> Leads thee, or where most needs, whether to wind   [215]
> The woodbine round this arbour, or direct
> The clasping ivy where to climb, while I
> In yonder spring of roses intermixed
> With myrtle, find what to redress till noon:
> For while so near each other thus all day   [220]
> Our task we choose, what wonder if so near
> Looks intervene and smiles, or object new
> Casual discourse draw on, which intermits
> Our day's work brought to little, though begun
> Early, and th' hour of supper comes unearned.   [225]
>   To whom mild answer Adam thus returned.
> Sole Eve, associate sole, to me beyond

Compare above all living creatures dear,
Well hast thou motioned, well thy thoughts employed
How we might best fulfill the work which here   [230]
God hath assigned us, nor of me shalt pass
Unpraised: for nothing lovelier can be found
In woman, than to study household good,
And good works in her husband to promote.
Yet not so strictly hath our Lord imposed   [235]
Labour, as to debar us when we need
Refreshment, whether food, or talk between,
Food of the mind, or this sweet intercourse
Of looks and smiles, for smiles from reason flow,
To brute denied, and are of love the food,   [240]
Love not the lowest end of human life.
For not to irksome toil, but to delight
He made us, and delight to reason joined.
These paths and bowers doubt not but our joint hands
Will keep from wilderness with ease, as wide   [245]
As we need walk, till younger hands ere long
Assist us: but if much convérse perhaps
Thee satiate, to short absence I could yield.
For solitude sometimes is best society,
And short retirement urges sweet return.   [250]
But other doubt possesses me, lest harm
Befall thee severed from me; for thou know'st
What hath been warned us, what malicious Foe
Envying our happiness, and of his own
Despairing, seeks to work us woe and shame   [255]
By sly assault; and somewhere nigh at hand
Watches, no doubt, with greedy hope to find
His wish and best advantage, us asunder,
Hopeless to circumvent us joined, where each
To other speedy aid might lend at need;   [260]
Whether his first design be to withdraw
Our fealty from God, or to disturb
Conjugal love, than which perhaps no bliss
Enjoyed by us excites his envy more;
Or this, or worse, leave not the faithful side   [265]
That gave thee being, still shades thee and protects.
The wife, where danger or dishonour lurks,
Safest and seemliest by her husband stays,
Who guards her, or with her the worst endures.
      To whom the virgin majesty of Eve,   [270]
As one who loves, and some unkindness meets,

With sweet austere composure thus replied.
    Offspring of Heav'n and earth, and all earth's lord,
That such an Enemy we have, who seeks
Our ruin, both by thee informed I learn,   [275]
And from the parting angel overheard
As in a shady nook I stood behind,
Just then returned at shut of evening flow'rs.
But that thou shouldst my firmness therefore doubt
To God or thee, because we have a foe   [280]
May tempt it, I expected not to hear.
His violence thou fear'st not, being such,
As we, not capable of death or pain,
Can either not receive, or can repel.
His fraud is then thy fear, which plain infers   [285]
Thy equal fear that my firm faith and love
Can by his fraud be shaken or seduced;
Thoughts, which how found they harbour in thy breast,
Adam, misthought of her to thee so dear?
    To whom with healing words Adam replied.   [290]
Daughter of God and man, immortal Eve,
For such thou art, from sin and blame entire:
Not diffident of thee do I dissuade
Thy absence from my sight, but to avoid
Th' attempt itself, intended by our Foe.   [295]
For he who tempts, though in vain, at least asperses
The tempted with dishonour foul, supposed
Not incorruptible of faith, not proof
Against temptation: thou thyself with scorn
And anger wouldst resent the offered wrong,   [300]
Though ineffectual found: misdeem not then,
If such affront I labour to avert
From thee alone, which on us both at once
The Enemy, though bold, will hardly dare,
Or daring, first on me th' assault shall light.   [305]
Nor thou his malice and false guile contemn;
Subtle he needs must be, who could seduce
Angels, nor think superfluous others' aid.
I from the influence of thy looks receive
Accéss in every virtue, in thy sight   [310]
More wise, more watchful, stronger, if need were
Of outward strength; while shame, thou looking on,
Shame to be overcome or over-reached
Would utmost vigour raise, and raised unite.
Why shouldst not thou like sense within thee feel   [315]

When I am present, and thy trial choose
With me, best witness of thy virtue tried.
     So spake domestic Adam in his care
And matrimonial love; but Eve, who thought
Less áttribúted to her faith sincere,   [320]
Thus her reply with accent sweet renewed.
     If this be our condition, thus to dwell
In narrow circuit straitened by a Foe,
Subtle or violent, we not endued
Single with like defence, wherever met,   [325]
How are we happy, still in fear of harm?
But harm precedes not sin: only our Foe
Tempting affronts us with his foul esteem
Of our integrity: his foul esteem
Sticks no dishonour on our front, but turns   [330]
Foul on himself; then wherefore shunned or feared
By us? Who rather double honour gain
From his surmise proved false, find peace within,
Favour from Heav'n, our witness from th' event.
And what is faith, love, virtue unassayed   [335]
Alone, without exterior help sustained?
Let us not then suspect our happy state
Left so imperfect by our Maker wise,
And not secure to single or combined.
Frail is our happiness, if this be so,   [340]
And Eden were no Eden thus exposed.
     To whom thus Adam fervently replied.
O woman, best are all things as the will
Of God ordained them; his creating hand
Nothing imperfect or deficient left   [345]
Of all that he created, much less man,
Or aught that might his happy state secure,
Secure from outward force; within himself
The danger lies, yet lies within his power:
Against his will he can receive no harm.   [350]
But God left free the will, for what obeys
Reason, is free, and reason he made right,
But bid her well beware, and still erect,
Lest by some fair appearing good surprised
She díctate false, and misinform the will   [355]
To do what God expressly hath forbid.
Not then mistrust, but tender love enjoins,
That I should mind thee oft, and mind thou me.
Firm we subsist, yet possible to swerve,

Since reason not impossibly may meet   [360]
Some specious object by the Foe suborned,
And fall into deception unaware,
Not keeping strictest watch, as she was warned.
Seek not temptation then, which to avoid
Were better, and most likely if from me   [365]
Thou sever not: trial will come unsought.
Wouldst thou approve thy constancy, approve
First thy obedience; th' other who can know,
Not seeing thee attempted, who attest?
But if thou think, trial unsought may find   [370]
Us both securer than thus warned thou seem'st,
Go; for thy stay, not free, absents thee more;
Go in thy native innocence, rely
On what thou hast of virtue, summon all,
For God towards thee hath done his part, do thine.   [375]
     So spake the patriarch of mankind, but Eve
Persisted, yet submiss, though last, replied.
     With thy permission, then, and thus forewarned
Chiefly by what thy own last reasoning words
Touched only, that our trial, when least sought,   [380]
May find us both perhaps far less prepared,
The willinger I go, nor much expect
A Foe so proud will first the weaker seek;
So bent, the more shall shame him his repulse.
Thus saying, from her husband's hand her hand   [385]
Soft she withdrew, and like a wood-nymph light
Oread or Dryad, or of Delia's train,
Betook her to the groves, but Delia's self
In gait surpassed and goddess-like deport,
Though not as she with bow and quiver armed,   [390]
But with such gard'ning tools as art yet rude,
Guiltless of fire had formed, or angels brought.
To Pales, or Pomona thus adorned,
Likeliest she seemed, Pomona when she fled
Vertumnus, or to Ceres in her prime,   [395]
Yet virgin of Proserpina from Jove.
Her long with ardent look his eye pursued
Delighted, but desiring more her stay.
Oft he to her his charge of quick return
Repeated, she to him as oft engaged   [400]
To be returned by noon amid the bow'r,
And all things in best order to invite
Noontide repast, or afternoon's repose.

O much deceived, much failing, hapless Eve,
Of thy presumed return! event perverse!   [405]
Thou never from that hour in Paradise
Found'st either sweet repast, or sound repose;
Such ambush hid among sweet flow'rs and shades
Waited with Hellish rancour imminent
To intercept thy way, or send thee back   [410]
Despoiled of innocence, of faith, of bliss.

4. Book IX. 780–1055

If the separation scene constitutes a moment of tragic error, then the
actual eating of the forbidden fruit is the tragic catastrophe. In the highly
dramatic passage reproduced below, in which Eve eats of the fruit and
then tempts Adam to do the same, Milton fills in the large gaps he finds
in the original Genesis account and veers in the process from any established exegetical tradition. For Milton, the Tree of Knowledge – placed
in the garden it seems for no other purpose than as an arbitrary sign of
Adam and Eve's trial of obedience – yields in fact only a 'fallacious fruit'
(IX. 1046). Its operation does not confer actual knowledge of good and
evil in an objective ethical sense by allowing Adam and Eve to know
right from wrong, but muddies innate goodness by distorting its moral
perspectives. Evil, as always in the poem, is a consequence of deprivation which leads to depravation, its knowledge inflicted rather than
simply acquired. As soon as Eve eats of the fruit, gorging on it 'without
restraint' (IX. 791), her sense of self is unsettled from its monistic, patriarchal equilibrium, as thoughts of envy and pride breed in her doubt
and anxiety. Suddenly Eve is not content with her subordinate state and
begins to echo Satan's rhetoric of defiance, contemplating for a brief
moment even direct rebellion against Adam and God, 'for inferior who
is free?' (IX. 835). The Miltonic answer provided throughout the poem
that freedom is a matter of reasoned choice and obedience, and not a
flattening of hierarchies, suddenly escapes her. Unlike Satan, however,
who is incapable of true feelings of love or amity, Eve finds that her love
for Adam is stronger than any impulse to rebel.

Love and marital devotion indeed suddenly emerge as the big tragic
themes of the climactic dialogue which leads to Adam's decision to fall
with Eve. In Milton's reimagining of the biblical myth, Adam heroically
falls for love. But is Adam's decision inevitable? In a much debated line,
the narrator informs us that having already decided to fall with Eve,
Adam turned to speak to her, 'Submitting to what seemed remediless'
(IX. 919). The word 'seemed' quietly points out that the remediless inev-

itability of Adam's choice to fall is only in Adam's despairing mind, and so the thought enters: perhaps there was another way out of the crisis that Adam, for any number of reasons, either suppressed or silently chose to ignore. Indeed both Eve after her fall and Adam before his reflect on a perplexing question which much exercised Christian theologians and exegetes: what if Adam had not been tempted to fall with Eve? Would God have then destroyed Eve while Adam remained forever alone, or would God have created for Adam a new, perhaps more obedient wife from yet another rib? An even wilder speculation turns this question another way: what if Adam actually chose at that moment of crisis to intercede on Eve's behalf before God and sacrificed himself, dying not with Eve, but for her? Could the unfallen Adam even be capable of such acts of selfless love, or are these reserved only to the loving mercy of the Son? It is the nature of 'what if' questions to be infuriatingly insoluble and in most cases utterly pointless, but these are questions which nevertheless cross the human mind, and they certainly seem to have crossed Milton's – what if the Fall could have been averted, if not for both humans, then at least for the man? For one thing, in mythological terms, the human race as we know it would not have existed. From our point of view, the Fall is an absolutely necessary and therefore happy tragedy; to try and envision our life without it is to think ourselves out of existence (for more on the paradox of the 'Fortunate Fall' see the commentary section below). However, to point this out betrays a lack of imagination which diminishes the complexity of Milton's poem. Both Eve and Adam, in different ways, consider for brief moments alternative possibilities and tease us with such thoughts as well. And when they finally recoil with horror at the suggestion, it is not because they are cognisant of being trapped in a theological paradox, or because they lack perhaps the imagination of the poet who gave them new life, but because, as Milton insists, they are utterly devoted to each other.

Once again Milton confounds us with a perplexing ethical riddle. Adam and Eve's 'collateral love' and devotion to each other cannot be in itself a bad thing – the narrator everywhere extols its prelapsarian virtues – and yet, it is this love as it finds expression through their individual free will that finally brings about their fall. As the narrator points out in one of the most famous lines of the poem, Adam eventually chooses to fall with Eve not because he is 'deceived' by her, but because he is 'fondly overcome with female charm' (IX. 999). The adverb 'fondly' is censorious and reminds us that there is a powerful argument here against which Adam's error is to be measured, but the logic of this argument is unequal to the overwhelming emotion with which Adam shows himself being overcome by Eve's female charm. The moving words he speaks to her moments before eating of the fruit are as noble as any lover ever spoke in literature: 'Our state cannot be severed, we are one, / One flesh; to lose thee were to lose myself' (IX. 958–9). Readers are justified at this moment to think of Satan, who defiantly declared in the opening book of the poem that it is 'Better to reign in Hell, than serve in Heav'n' (I. 263). What Adam is saying is disquietingly similar – it is better to love in the fallen world than remain forever alone in paradise. Take away love and companionship and paradise too can become just another kind of hell. Adam and Eve's dire trespass undeniably debases the sort of intellectual, chaste love Milton elevates as an ideal throughout the poem. After Adam eats of the apple and the 'mortal sin / Original' (IX. 1003–4) is completed, the first human couple suddenly discovers the guilt (and joys) of concupiscence, followed by bickering and recriminations. But Milton also demonstrates on a deep poetic level that even the noblest intellectual love simply could not have withstood the test of paradise. Perhaps it was never meant to.

> So saying, her rash hand in evil hour [780]
> Forth reaching to the fruit, she plucked, she ate:
> Earth felt the wound, and Nature from her seat
> Sighing through all her works gave signs of woe,
> That all was lost. Back to the thicket slunk
> The guilty serpent, and well might, for Eve [785]
> Intent now wholly on her taste, naught else
> Regarded, such delight till then, as seemed,
> In fruit she never tasted, whether true
> Or fancied so, through expectation high
> Of knowledge, nor was Godhead from her thought. [790]
> Greedily she engorged without restraint,
> And knew not eating death: satiate at length,
> And heightened as with wine, jocund and boon,
> Thus to herself she pleasingly began.
> O sov'reign, virtuous, precious of all trees [795]
> In Paradise, of operation blest
> To sapience, hitherto obscured, infamed,
> And thy fair fruit let hang, as to no end
> Created; but henceforth my early care,
> Not without song, each morning, and due praise [800]
> Shall tend thee, and the fertile burden ease
> Of thy full branches offered free to all;
> Till dieted by thee I grow mature
> In knowledge, as the gods who all things know;

Though others envy what they cannot give; [805]
For had the gift been theirs, it had not here
Thus grown. Experience, next to thee I owe,
Best guide; not following thee, I had remained
In ignorance, thou open'st wisdom's way,
And giv'st accéss, though secret she retire. [810]
And I perhaps am secret; Heav'n is high,
High and remote to see from thence distinct
Each thing on earth; and other care perhaps
May have diverted from continual watch
Our great Forbidder, safe with all his spies [815]
About him. But to Adam in what sort
Shall I appear? shall I to him make known
As yet my change, and give him to partake
Full happiness with me, or rather not,
But keep the odds of knowledge in my power [820]
Without copartner? so to add what wants
In female sex, the more to draw his love,
And render me more equal, and perhaps,
A thing not undesirable, sometime
Superior; for inferior who is free? [825]
This may be well; but what if God have seen,
And death ensue? then I shall be no more,
And Adam wedded to another Eve,
Shall live with her enjoying, I extinct;
A death to think. Confirmed then I resolve, [830]
Adam shall share with me in bliss or woe:
So dear I love him, that with him all deaths
I could endure, without him live no life.
    So saying, from the tree her step she turned,
But first low reverence done, as to the power [835]
That dwelt within, whose presence had infused
Into the plant sciential sap, derived
From nectar, drink of gods. Adam the while
Waiting desirous her return, had wove
Of choicest flow'rs a garland to adorn [840]
Her tresses, and her rural labours crown,
As reapers oft are wont their harvest queen.
Great joy he promised to his thoughts, and new
Solace in her return, so long delayed;
Yet oft his heart, divine of something ill, [845]
Misgave him; he the falt'ring measure felt;
And forth to meet her went, the way she took
That morn when first they parted; by the Tree

Of Knowledge he must pass, there he her met,
Scarce from the tree returning; in her hand   [850]
A bough of fairest fruit that downy smiled,
New gathered, and ambrosial smell diffused.
To him she hasted, in her face excuse
Came prologue, and apology to prompt,
Which with bland words at will she thus addressed.   [855]
    Hast thou not wondered, Adam, at my stay?
Thee I have missed, and thought it long, deprived
Thy presence, agony of love till now
Not felt, nor shall be twice, for never more
Mean I to try, what rash untried I sought,   [860]
The pain of absence from thy sight. But strange
Hath been the cause, and wonderful to hear:
This tree is not as we are told, a tree
Of danger tasted, nor to evil unknown
Op'ning the way, but of divine effect   [865]
To open eyes, and make them gods who taste;
And hath been tasted such: the serpent wise,
Or not restrained as we, or not obeying,
Hath eaten of the fruit, and is become,
Not dead, as we are threatened, but thenceforth   [870]
Endued with human voice and human sense,
Reasoning to admiration, and with me
Persuasively hath so prevailed, that I
Have also tasted, and have also found
Th' effects to correspond, opener mine eyes,   [875]
Dim erst, dilated spirits, ampler heart,
And growing up to godhead; which for thee
Chiefly I sought, without thee can despise.
For bliss, as thou hath part, to me is bliss,
Tedious, unshared with thee, and odious soon.   [880]
Thou therefore also taste, that equal lot
May join us, equal joy, as equal love;
Lest thou not tasting, different degree
Disjoin us, and I then too late renounce
Deity for thee, when Fate will not permit.   [885]
    Thus Eve with count'nance blithe her story told;
But in her cheek distemper flushing glowed.
On th' other side, Adam, soon as he heard
The fatal trespass done by Eve, amazed,
Astonied stood and blank, while horror chill   [890]
Ran through his veins, and all his joints relaxed;
From his slack hand the garland wreathed for Eve

Down dropped, and all the faded roses shed:
Speechless he stood and pale, till thus at length
First to himself he inward silence broke.   [895]
     O fairest of Creation, last and best
Of all God's works, creature in whom excelled
Whatever can to sight or thought be formed,
Holy, divine, good, amiable or sweet!
How art thou lost, how on a sudden lost,   [900]
Defaced, deflow'red, and now to death devote?
Rather how hast thou yielded to transgress
The strict forbiddance, how to violate
The sacred fruit forbidd'n! Some cursèd fraud
Of Enemy hath beguiled thee, yet unknown,   [905]
And me with thee hath ruined, for with thee
Certain my resolution is to die;
How can I live without thee, how forgo
Thy sweet convérse and love so dearly joined,
To live again in these wild woods forlorn?   [910]
Should God create another Eve, and I
Another rib afford, yet loss of thee
Would never from my heart; no no, I feel
The link of nature draw me: flesh of flesh,
Bone of my bone thou art, and from thy state   [915]
Mine never shall be parted, bliss or woe.
     So having said, as one from sad dismay
Recomforted, and after thoughts disturbed
Submitting to what seemed remédiless,
Thus in calm mood his words to Eve he turned.   [920]
     Bold deed thou hast presumed, advent'rous Eve,
And peril great provoked, who thus hath dared
Had it been only coveting to eye
That sacred fruit, sacred to abstinence,
Much more to taste it under ban to touch.   [925]
But past who can recall, or done undo?
Not God omnipotent, nor Fate, yet so
Perhaps thou shalt not die, perhaps the fact
Is not so heinous now, foretasted fruit,
Profaned first by the serpent, by him first   [930]
Made common and unhallowed ere our taste;
Nor yet on him found deadly; he yet lives,
Lives, as thou saidst, and gains to live as man
Higher degree of life, inducement strong
To us, as likely tasting to attain   [935]
Proportional ascent, which cannot be

But to the gods, or angels demi-gods.
Nor can I think that God, Creator wise,
Though threat'ning, will in earnest so destroy
Us his prime creatures, dignified so high,   [940]
Set over all his works, which in our Fall,
For us created, needs with us must fail,
Dependent made; so God shall uncreate,
Be frustrate, do, undo, and labour lose,
Not well conceived of God, who though his power   [945]
Creation could repeat, yet would be loath
Us to abolish, lest the Adversary
Triúmph and say; Fickle their state whom God
Most favours, who can please him long? Me first
He ruined, now mankind; whom will he next?   [950]
Matter of scorn, not to be given the Foe.
However I with thee have fixed my lot,
Certain to undergo like doom; if death
Consort with thee, death is to me as life;
So forcible within my heart I feel   [955]
The bond of nature draw me to my own,
My own in thee, for what thou art is mine;
Our state cannot be severed, we are one,
One flesh; to lose thee were to lose myself.
  So Adam, and thus Eve to him replied.   [960]
O glorious trial of exceeding love,
Illustrious evidence, example high!
Engaging me to emulate, but short
Of thy perfection, how shall I attain,
Adam, from whose dear side I boast me sprung,   [965]
And gladly of our union hear thee speak,
One heart, one soul in both; whereof good proof
This day affords, declaring thee resolved,
Rather than death of aught than death more dread
Shall separate us, linked in love so dear,   [970]
To undergo with me one guilt, one crime,
If any be, of tasting this fair fruit,
Whose virtue, for of good still good proceeds,
Direct, or by occasion hath presented
This happy trial of thy love, which else   [975]
So eminently never had been known.
Were it I thought death menaced would ensue
This my attempt, I would sustain alone
The worst, and not persuade thee, rather die
Deserted, than oblige thee with a fact   [980]

Pernicious to thy peace, chiefly assured
Remarkably so late of thy so true,
So faithful love unequalled; but I feel
Far otherwise th' event, not death, but life
Augmented, opened eyes, new hopes, new joys,   [985]
Taste so divine, that what of sweet before
Hath touched my sense, flat seems to this, and harsh.
On my experience, Adam, freely taste,
And fear of death deliver to the winds.
    So saying, she embraced him, and for joy   [990]
Tenderly wept, much won that he his love
Had so ennobled, as of choice to incur
Divine displeasure for her sake, or death.
In recompense (for such compliance bad
Such recompense best merits) from the bough   [995]
She gave him of that fair enticing fruit
With liberal hand: he scrupled not to eat
Against his better knowledge, not deceived,
But fondly overcome with female charm.
Earth trembled from her entrails, as again   [1000]
In pangs, and Nature gave a second groan;
Sky loured, and muttering thunder, some sad drops
Wept at completing of the mortal sin
Original; while Adam took no thought,
Eating his fill, nor Eve to iterate   [1005]
Her former trespass feared, the more to soothe
Him with her loved society, that now
As with new wine intoxicated both
They swim in mirth, and fancy that they feel
Divinity within them breeding wings   [1010]
Wherewith to scorn the earth: but that false fruit
Far other operation first displayed,
Carnal desire inflaming; he on Eve
Began to cast lascivious eyes, she him
As wantonly repaid; in lust they burn: [1015]
Till Adam thus gan Eve to dalliance move.
    Eve, now I see thou art exact of taste,
And elegant, of sapience no small part,
Since to each meaning savour we apply,
And palate call judicious; I the praise   [1020]
Yield thee, so well this day thou hast purveyed.
Much pleasure we have lost, while we abstained
From this delightful fruit, nor known till now
True relish, tasting; if such pleasure be

In things to us forbidden, it might be wished,   [1025]
For this one tree had been forbidden ten.
But come, so well refreshed, now let us play,
As meet is, after such delicious fare;
For never did thy beauty since the day
I saw thee first and wedded thee, adorned   [1030]
With all perfections, so inflame my sense
With ardour to enjoy thee, fairer now
Than ever, bounty of this virtuous tree.
    So said he, and forbore not glance or toy
Of amorous intent, well understood   [1035]
Of Eve, whose eyes darted contagious fire.
Her hand he seized, and to a shady bank,
Thick overhead with verdant roof embow'red
He led her nothing loath; flow'rs were the couch,
Pansies, and violets, and asphodel,   [1040]
And hyacinth, earth's freshest softest lap.
There they their fill of love and love's disport
Took largely, of their mutual guilt the seal,
The solace of their sin, till dewy sleep
Oppressed them, wearied with their amorous play.   [1045]
Soon as the force of that fallacious fruit,
That with exhilarating vapour bland
About their spirits had played, and inmost powers
Made err, was now exhaled, and grosser sleep
Bred of unkindly fumes, with conscious dreams   [1050]
Encumbered, now had left them, up they rose
As from unrest, and each the other viewing,
Soon found their eyes how opened, and their minds
How darkened; innocence, that as a veil
Had shadowed them from knowing ill, was gone;   [1055]

Commentary and analysis

Concepts and themes

To this day Roman Catholics sing during the mass of the Easter Vigil a Latin hymn, the *Exultet*, which includes the following verses (translated from the Latin): 'O truly necessary sin of Adam, which the death of Christ has blotted out! O happy fault that merited such and so great a Redeemer!'[13] The words 'happy fault' translate the Latin 'felix culpa', more commonly translated as 'Fortunate Fall'. The so-called paradox of the Fortunate Fall is very ancient and was developed as a theological argument in the teachings of the early Latin Fathers, St Ambrose and St Augustine, who coined the phrase. Both Fathers reasoned that the fall of Adam and Eve must be necessarily a fortunate event from a Christian point of view because it secured for humanity the sacrifice of Christ (and by implication the miracle of the incarnation as well), and therefore far greater felicity than was possible before the Fall. Where before the Fall all that was possible for man was a blissful existence on a par with angelic perfection, the gift of Christ's sacrifice promises ultimate union with the Godhead itself through the bounty of God's grace. The dry logic of calling the fall 'fortunate' is of course perverse and it raises numerous insoluble questions about God's providence, especially since it implies that a foreknowing God deliberately engineered the Fall to demonstrate his love and mercy in bringing about a greater good to man. This belief lends itself to the argument that God always finds ways to bring good out of evil. Milton too is hostage to this idea up to a point. Towards the end of the poem, after Adam learns from the archangel Michael about the Son's offered sacrifice and the promise of 'far happier place / Than this of Eden, and far happier days' (XII. 464–5), he breaks out in a hymn of gratitude:

> O goodness infinite, goodness immense!
> That all this good of evil shall produce,
> And evil turn to good; more wonderful
> That that which by creation first brought forth
> Light out of darkness! full of doubt I stand,
> Whether I should repent me now of sin
> By me done and occasioned, or rejoice
> Much more, that much more good thereof shall spring,
> To God more glory, more good will to men
> From God, and over wrath grace shall abound.
> (XII. 469–78)

Adam is not the only one to be 'full of doubt' when reflecting on this quandary and it is significant that the angel quietly avoids Adam's question which is in fact not at all rhetorical. Adam is not sure, given the paradox of the Fortunate Fall, whether he should now repent, and it is quite evident Milton was unsure too.

Milton's ambivalence about this paradox is evident from the very opening lines of the poem, which allude to the fortunate inevitability which leads from Adam's disobedience to Jesus' redemption of the original trespass:

> Of *man*'s first disobedience, and the fruit
> Of that forbidden tree, whose mortal taste

Brought death into the world, and all our woe,
With loss of Eden, till one greater *man*
Restore us, and regain the blissful seat
(I. 1–5, my emphases)

Adam and Jesus are linked in the opening lines of the poem typologi-
cally and graphically through the word 'man', but these lines also betray
Milton's unhappiness with the 'fortunate' paradigm otherwise implicit
in this familiar biblical typology and registered by Adam towards the
end of the epic. For Milton, there is nothing happy or fortunate about
the Fall in its immediate and felt consequences – as the narrator declares
at the outset of Book IX, it is a tragedy of 'foul distrust, and breach /
Disloyal on the part of man, revolt, / And disobedience' which 'brought
into this world a world of woe' (IX. 6–11). As we have seen throughout the commentary so far, the 'woe' implied here and at the opening
of the poem extends to every aspect of human life and existence, from
personal and domestic relationships to political, religious, and spiritual
concerns in the wider human community. Moreover, while the final
redemption given as a promise to all Christians gives hope for a better
life in the remote apocalyptic future, it is a future which is nevertheless
remote. The word 'till' in the opening lines quoted above weighs heavily
on the projected optimism: a 'greater man' than Adam will one day
'Restore us', but not for a very long time indeed. Milton strongly implies
throughout the poem that the world in its present state of sinfulness is
certainly not ready for such spiritual restoration. *Paradise Lost* belongs
as a narrative poem only to the fallen present and what it offers for
its 'fit' readers is a lament as well as possible remedies which can help
prepare mankind for its eventual redemption.

The paradox of the Fortunate Fall continually interferes, therefore,
with Milton's didactic impulse in the poem to teach and instruct because
it risks breeding complacency. Milton avoids this by reducing the extent
of the paradox and promoting instead the idea that if the Fall is fortunate, its rewards have to be secured in the fallen world through the
lessons it teaches. This explains the strong presence of education as a
central theme in Milton's portrayal of paradise. Milton deeply cared
about education. He tutored his nephews at home and put to paper his
thoughts on the theory and practice of an ideal education in a short
treatise commissioned by the humanist educationalist Samuel Hartlib
and first published in 1644 as *Of Education*. In this short but ambitious
treatise Milton adopts the common humanist notion that education in
a wide range of skills, both intellectual and physical, is necessary to
correct the deficiencies in man's intuitive divine knowledge after the Fall:

'The end then of learning is to repair the ruins of our first parents by regaining to know God aright'.[14] Strangely, however, education flourishes in Milton's paradise even before the Fall, where knowledge of God, unlike knowledge of the flora and fauna of the garden for example, is not intuitive but acquired. In Book VIII (passage 2 above) Adam relates how soon after being created he could 'readily' use language to name and classify objects around him, but that he could not use the same intuitive knowledge to discern who or what he was and who created him; in other words, while Adam could name the animals and plants of paradise, he could not name himself or his creator:

> But who I was, or where, or from what cause,
> Knew not; to speak I tried, and forthwith spake,
> My tongue obeyed and readily could name
> Whate'er I saw.
> (VIII. 270–3)

Like Eve who dotes on her own reflection in the pool, Adam also initially lacks any sense of himself and runs the risk of idolatry when he obsequiously addresses the sun, the first thing he sees in the sky, as 'fair light' (VIII. 273). Unlike Eve, however, Adam is bereft of the idolater's reflexivity instinct, intuitively understanding that he was created by a 'great Maker . . . In goodness and in power pre-eminent' (VIII. 278–9) and that he would require therefore the firm, guiding hand of an educator. Adam awakens, therefore, with a thirst not for knowledge per se, but for education.

The Fall of course changes things. Raphael and Michael, the two angelic teachers before and after the Fall, are very different in their pedagogical approach. Where Raphael provides necessary knowledge literally and directly so that Adam and Eve might not fall (or at least to render them 'inexcusable' should they fall), Michael speaks to the now fallen humans in the stern voice of prophecy and correction, setting out the path for re-education after the Fall, when direct knowledge of God and his ways is now dimmed by sinfulness. But the overriding idea prevails that the need for proper education is not itself endemic of the Fall, but is in fact a precondition of human createdness consequent on God's decree of free will. As we have seen in the passages reproduced above, Milton continually projects ideals about human relationships and liberty onto the prelapsarian utopia of Eden, which he then shows being shattered by error and disobedience. The entire sequence of paradise, and through it the poem as a whole, is in this respect an ongoing learning experience in which the poet acts as our educator. Education is what drives and stimulates the ability of the rational mind to make right ethical choices, and by writing this idea into the very poetics of the poem both before and after the Fall Milton in effect trains his readers to understand their role as fallen human beings in heuristic terms. In the final analysis, Milton does not merely hope to find a 'fit audience . . . though few' (VII. 31) of likeminded readers, but actively seeks to breed such fitness through a process of educational engagement.

Style and form
In the sections of hell and heaven we focused mostly on the style which distinguishes the tone of such diametrically opposed characters as Satan and God and the imagery which occasionally frames such speeches. In paradise, however, the style which gives substance to Adam's and Eve's respective characters and the setting of the garden more generally is more diffused and various, encompassing a much wider emotional range, from lyric joy and pastoral charm to elegiac sorrow and deep tragedy. Occasionally, faint echoes of the grand sublime attending satanic rhetoric in hell or divine decrees in heaven are also heard in Milton's paradise. Echoes of satanic guile, for example, insinuate themselves into Eve's gullible innocence before the Fall, adding to the deeply ambivalent imagery which already surrounds her with a dangerous aura of over-determined suggestiveness. What is only implied before the Fall, then breaks out as the symptom of a darker contamination after Eve succumbs to the serpent's temptation and eats of the forbidden fruit. Her innocence stripped away, Eve begins to express herself in overtly serpentine, suspiciously satanic sentences. Take, for example, Eve's words to Adam soon after she returns to him having eaten from the Tree of Knowledge:

> Thee I have missed, and thought it long, deprived
> Thy presence, agony of love till now
> Not felt, nor shall be twice, for never more
> Mean I to try, what rash untried I sought,
> The pain of absence from thy sight.
> (IX. 857–61)

The choppy, halting syntax of these lines reflects Eve's distraught state of mind. Where previously Eve was capable of genuine tenderness and simple, though chiastic expressions of love as in 'Part of my soul I seek thee, and thee claim / My other half' (IV. 487–8), now we hear for the first time not of 'love' but of its 'agony'. Indeed, the word 'love', elsewhere so crucial for inscribing the prelapsarian marital harmony of the first human couple, is drowned here in a typically satanic crescendo of negatives and false reversals, and finally sinks under the weight of such hollow words as 'missed', 'deprived' and 'absence'. This language captures something of Satan's despair we encountered in his soliloquies earlier in Book IV, but the resulting speech in Eve's case is never sinister, only sad. When Satan speaks of possible love when he first lays eyes on Adam and Eve (IV. 363), it is a despairing love from the start, but Eve's love, even in agony, is not any less real or heartfelt than it was before her transgression. In other words, stylistic effects in the poem depend on the accumulated effect of context, creating fine distinctions and nuances by linking many different passages in complex thematic patterns. As critic Balachandra Rajan remarked in a famous essay,

> The complexity of Milton's epic is less one of surface than of reverberation. It arises not so much from the immediate contexts, as from the connexion of that context to other contexts and eventually to the context of the whole poem and of the cosmic order drawn into and recreated within it.[15]

Situated at the centre of the created world between heaven and hell, paradise is also at the centre of the poem, and it functions as its main stylistic echoing chamber. Just as Satan's rhetoric reverberates in Eve's fallen tones, so Adam occasionally exhibits something of the poise, rational aloofness and preachy rhetorical rhythms we find with God's speeches in heaven. Here, for example, are the words of Adam when lecturing to Eve in Book IV about the merit of labour and rest in paradise:

> Fair consort, th' hour
> Of night, and all things now retired to rest
> Mind us of like repose, since God hath set
> Labour and rest, as day and night to men
> Successive, and the timely dew of sleep
> Now falling with soft slumb'rous weight inclines
> Our eye-lids; other creatures all day long
> Rove idle unemployed, and less need rest;
> Man hath his daily work of body or mind
> Appointed, which declares his dignity,
> And the regard of Heav'n on all his ways;
> While other animals unactive range,
> And of their doings God takes no account.
> (IV. 610–22)

The tone here is measured and superior. The quiet rhythm of what is in fact a long, complex sentence exudes the required sense of control and calm, accentuated by the strong monosyllabic line endings of 'rest' and 'set'. The style here captures the idea that if there is 'labour' in paradise it is always, as Adam says a line later, 'pleasant' (IV. 625). Here too, however, stylistic echoes of heaven and divine speech create distinctions rather than simple correlations. Significantly, unlike God Adam hardly ever resorts to the use of abstract nouns and concepts. Words such as 'work', 'rest' and 'labour', while potentially abstract in some contexts, assume a concreteness in relation to the interaction of 'body or mind' in the life of the first human couple. Abstract nouns can be slippery things to define. Most readers, for example, will agree that when God the Father speaks in Book III 'Of true allegiance, constant faith or love' (III. 104), the nouns in question are abstract in the extreme, but somehow less abstract when he next speaks of man's 'reason' and 'will'. Part of the aim of Adam and Eve's education before the Fall is to render such abstract nouns as 'obedience', 'faith' and 'love' intelligible. The forbidden Tree of Knowledge acts in this context as a concrete object, or sign, which anchors the meaning of many such abstract concepts in paradise before the Fall. Crucially, the one abstract noun prelapsarian Adam cannot fathom, notwithstanding his education, is 'death'. Adam says of the Tree of Knowledge that it is 'planted by the Tree of Life, / So near grows death to life, whate'er death is, / Some dreadful thing no doubt' (IV. 424–6). Although it seems odd that Adam should understand what 'life' is and be thankful for it while not understanding the meaning of 'death', the theological idea here is fairly straightforward: before the Fall 'death' can only exist 'near' life as an abstraction or a threat attached to an arbitrary sign like a forbidden tree; after the Fall, 'death' will assume an all too concrete presence in human existence, not just as the abstract antonym of 'life', but as its material negation.

These isolated observations about the language and style of Adam and Eve before and after the Fall point to a greater stylistic and thematic design calculated to confront the reader with the tragic enormity of the loss of paradise. Critics such as Ricks, Rajan, Fish, Stein and especially Leonard (see bibliography) have all written eloquently on the stylistic and idiomatic nuances which generate a sense of elegiac loss throughout the recreation of paradise in the poem. One of the most famous and much debated examples for this practice is the description of the river running through paradise with 'mazy error under pendent shades' (IV. 239). 'Error' is a word which carries undeniably negative connotations, even though it is clear that in paradise before the Fall it should simply mean 'wandering about irregularly'. For Ricks, the word 'error' is a 'reminder of the Fall, in that it takes us back to a time when there were no infected words because there were no infected actions',[16] while for Fish, such words contaminate the poem with sin, leaving the reader 'no choice but to acknowledge himself as the source [of the sinfulness] and to lament'.[17] Leonard, in a detailed reconsideration of this discussion, disagrees with Fish and argues instead that while 'Milton never lets us forget that Paradise is lost, [. . .] he does permit us sometimes to forget ourselves', qualifying our sense of shared bliss with the emerging picture of Edenic bliss, but never excluding us from it.[18] Many more examples of such words as 'error' can be brought forward and analyzed, and their possible 'fallen' connotations do indeed, as Leonard suggests, cover a very wide range of registers beyond the simplistic one of sin. For example, when Adam instructs Eve that their joint gardening duty is 'to reform / Yon flow'ry arbours' (IV. 625–6), the verb 'reform' does not introduce the false ring of a fallen political discourse, or bait the reader's sinfulness, but positively reinforces the political allegory which the husbandry of the Garden of Eden before the Fall opens up to in the poem. Such suggestiveness and the resulting metaphorical fecundity of paradise remind us that style is never a superficial decorative dimension in *Paradise Lost*. Almost every word Milton chooses is carefully considered and poetically justified (even if the dry logic of grammar and sense occasionally imply redundancy), while the poem's central thematic concerns are never imposed on the poetry, but are deeply implicated in its material fabric.

The historical-political context

We have already noted that Milton projects onto the pre- and postlapsarian visions of paradise complex theological and political arguments about the realisation of true liberty and conjugal harmony in the domestic sphere. Marriage, or more precisely the right of a man to seek divorce in an unhappy marriage, was a topic Milton worried about earlier in life after his first wife, Mary Powell, abandoned him and returned to her father's house soon after the wedding (the couple would not be reunited for more than two years). The reasons for Milton's early marital problems remain speculative and are the subject of much historical gossip. What *is* known is that Milton, finding himself married but without a wife while the civil war raged around him, appealed to Parliament and the Westminster Assembly of Divines in a prose treatise entitled *The Doctrine and Discipline of Divorce* to allow a man to divorce his wife and remarry on grounds of intellectual incompatibility resulting in loneliness or desertion. In the event, Milton ended up writing no less than four, highly unorthodox divorce tracts which brought down on him the opprobrium and anger of the Assembly and bracketed him with other sectarians and Independents on the radical fringes of English society at the time. According to English canon law (which in this case the Assembly sought to uphold), a complete dissolution of the marriage bond allowing the parties to remarry was only possible if there was threat of polygamy or incest, or if it could be shown that one of the parties entered the marriage contract under duress without giving their consent. Even proven cases of adultery could only enforce a divorce from 'bed and board' but not dissolve the sacred marriage bond instituted by Christ. Arguing from the bitter circumstances of his personal domestic crisis, a frustrated and angry Milton ingeniously argued that Christ's and Paul's otherwise very clear pronouncements against divorce in the Gospels should not be taken literally but made subject to the laws of Christian charity. Anchoring his exegetical polemic in Genesis 2: 18 ('And the Lord God said, It is not good that the man should be alone; I will make him an help meet for him'), Milton argued that since the purpose of marriage was to alleviate loneliness in fit companionship, it was unchristian and uncharitable to allow any marriage to continue if these conditions were not met. Eventually, Mary and John Milton were reconciled, but the argument born of the original marital crisis, filtered at the time through the larger dissolution of contract between king and parliament and the growing rift between the Presbyterian Assembly and the Independents, remained a mainstay of Milton's ideology, and re-emerged years later in the recreation of Genesis in *Paradise Lost*.[19]

The presence of marriage in Milton's paradise before the Fall essentially politicises Eden. Adam and Eve's 'happy nuptial league' (IV. 339) represents not just the ideal married state as Milton saw it, where a wife has to be an obedient intellectual helpmeet to her husband, but also the ideal human household in the broadest sense possible, including any human co-habitation in a city or a state where masculine principles of rationality and hierarchal liberty must hold sway. In disobeying God and committing a primeval act of idolatry by eating from the Tree of Knowledge, Adam and Eve sunder the ideal spiritual and intellectual union which they shared. The Fall itself becomes in this context a type of divorce, or dissolution of the ideal union between man and God, and man and wife. It also sets the terms under which any marriage union or social contract after the Fall has to be measured. In this context, it is important to note that many of the political distinctions written into the setting of paradise depend, curiously enough, on the politics of sexual relations. In his earlier divorce tracts, Milton assumed an austere tone in denigrating those who enter marriage solely for the purpose of enjoying legitimised sexual intercourse. In seeking to emphasise the merit of intellectual conjugal love over mere carnal attraction, Milton had to subordinate the important command of procreation to that of companionship, going as far as calling in the *Doctrine and Discipline* the act of procreation when enjoyed for its own sake a 'quintessence of an excrement'.[20] Milton, however, probably did not really believe this, and was only pandering in this case to the puritanical sensibilities of the Presbyterian divines he was appealing to. On the contrary, in *Paradise Lost* the narrator celebrates Adam and Eve's prelapsarian sexuality, where having dutifully prayed to God, the first human married couple enjoys 'the rites / Mysterious of connubial love'. Moreover, the narrator then goes on to defend these 'rites' against 'hypocrites' who 'defam[e] as impure what God declares / Pure, and commands to some, leaves free to all' (IV. 742–7). Such love, which ought to find healthy sexual expression, is founded not in lust, but, as the narrator goes on to say, 'in reason, loyal, just, and pure' (IV. 755). These ideas extend far beyond pre- and postlapsarian sexuality and tie into the poem's main argument about true as opposed to false liberty. Before the Fall Adam and Eve enter their nuptial bower 'Handed' (IV. 739) as equal companions enjoying true liberty within their marital union, but after the Fall we hear how, inflamed by sudden lust, Adam 'seize[s]' Eve by the hand, dragging her 'nothing loath' (IX. 1039) into a 'shady bank' (IX. 1037) where they consummate not their marital union, but their mutual carnal attraction. In *Paradise Lost*, the Fall and the loss of liberty it entails debase human desires. Milton insists that the resulting slavery of the rational faculties to sensual appetite and passions leaves humanity in a state of naked shame divested of 'native righteousness' (IX. 1056). The political attitude *Paradise Lost* seeks to engender in its intended readers is consequently one where 'righteousness', though no longer native, is re-merited, re-acquired, and put to good use in re-forming the Christian world according to the utopian model of life in paradise Adam and Eve erroneously and so tragically lost.

Notes

1. The full quotation runs: 'The reason Milton wrote in fetters when he wrote of Angels and God, and at liberty when of Devils and Hell, is because he was a true Poet and of the Devil's party without knowing it', William Blake, *The Marriage of Heaven and Hell* (*c*.1790), quoted in Timothy C. Miller (ed.), *The Critical Response to John Milton's* Paradise Lost (Westport, CT: Greenwood Press, 1997), p. 117. What is especially significant about Blake's sentiment is its typically Romantic association of the purpose and power of 'true' poetry with the freedom of the imagination that comes with being a member of the 'Devil's party'. For Philip Pullman's comparable thoughts on *Paradise Lost* students can consult his introduction to the illustrated hardback republication of the Orgel

and Goldberg edition of the poem, John Milton, *Paradise Lost*, introduced by Philip Pullman (Oxford: Oxford University Press, 2005).

2. Milton's nephew Edward Phillips noted in his early biography of his uncle that Milton showed him and others a draft of what are now lines 32–41 in Book IV 'several Years before the Poem was begun' as the 'beginning' of a tragedy. See Darbishire, *Early Lives*, pp. 72–3.

3. Coleridge coined this famous phrase in a note he wrote for his lecture on *Othello*, where he commented on Iago's 'put money in thy purse' speech, 'the motive-hunting of motiveless Malignity – how awful!', *Lectures 1808–1819 on Literature*, 2 vols, ed. R. A. Foakes, in *The Collected Works of Samuel Taylor Coleridge*, 16 vols, general ed. Kathleen Coburn (Princeton: Princeton University Press, 1987), vol. 5, p. 315.

4. The earliest recorded attribution of this paradox to Epicurus is in the Latin writings of the early Church Father Lactantius, where this passage is already coloured by Christian terminology and concerns. 'Evil', in Latin 'malum', has no direct corollary in Greek and it is doubtful whether in the Greek original the paradox meant the same thing. Epicurus was not concerned with proving the 'evil' of the gods, but only their indifference.

5. Empson argues that Satan logically dismisses with 'splendid intellectual energy' the Son's elevation as a 'gross piece of nepotism' (*Milton's God*, p. 83).

6. Samuel Johnson, 'Prefaces, Biographical and Critical, to the Works of the English Poets', in *Samuel Johnson: The Major Works*, ed. Donald Greene (Oxford: Oxford University Press, 1984), pp. 711–12.

7. The idea that latent Gnostic ideas shape Milton's representation of the Trinity in *Paradise Lost* is the central argument of A. D. Nuttall's *The Alternative Trinity: Gnostic Heresy in Marlowe, Milton, and Blake* (Oxford: Clarendon Press, 1998).

8. Fallon, *Milton's Peculiar Grace*, p. 201.

9. *CPW*, vi, p. 134.

10. Fish, *Surprised by Sin*, p. 64.

11. *CPW*, vi, p. 134.

12. Northrop Frye, *Five Essays*, p. 66.

13. *The Complete Office of Holy Week According to the Roman Missal and Breviary, in Latin and English* (1875), pp. 427–8.

14. *CPW*, ii, pp. 366–7.

15. Balachandra Rajan, 'The Style of *Paradise Lost*', in C. A. Patrides (ed.), *Milton's Epic Poetry: Essays on* Paradise Lost *and* Paradise Regained (Harmondsworth: Penguin, 1967), pp. 276–97, at p. 296.

16. Ricks, *Milton's Grand Style*, p. 110.

17. Fish, *Surprised by Sin*, p. 136.

18. Leonard, *Naming in Paradise*, p. 234.

19. For more on the political context of Milton's divorce tracts students might well consider Sharon Achinstein's essay in the *Oxford Handbook of Milton*, ed. McDowell and Smith, pp. 174–85.

20. *CPW*, ii, p. 240.

Chapter 3

Teaching the Text

The following chapter aims to provide teachers coming to *Paradise Lost* for the first time a number of possible approaches for teaching the poem to undergraduate and possibly graduate students as well. *Paradise Lost* is a great teaching text, not least because the idea of instruction and education is at the heart of the poem itself. Indeed, there is no better way to gain an in-depth understanding of the poem than to teach it. While a teacher should always be prepared to bring a great deal of background knowledge to the teaching of such a complex poem, it is often the case that in key areas the poem takes over even from the most prepared teacher. The polemical energies contained in *Paradise Lost* are indeed so great that they tend to generate class debates which quickly take on a life of their own, and then it is just a matter of managing and directing the discussions to areas a teacher wants to focus on. Resistance to, and even initial dislike of the poem are not uncommon therefore. The teacher should not shy away from such reactions or dismiss them, but allow for students holding such views to defend them. Students of the poem should be pushed to articulate more forcefully and precisely any claim they make with reference to key passages from the text. As long as the text remains at the centre of discussion, almost any point of view should be fair play.

The best general approach to teaching *Paradise Lost*, therefore, is to let it do most of the work for you. My own experiences in this regard have always proved, for example, that as soon as you bring into play questions relating to the right or wrong of Milton's God and Satan most students are bound to have very strong opinions, even if they do not yet fully understand the finer points of the poem's theology. When I first started teaching *Paradise Lost* I always assigned students the essay I was assigned myself as a student: 'Do you think Milton succeeds in justifying the ways of God to men?' There is nothing like this deceptively simple and often very personal question to get the discussion of the poem's main ideas going, but I soon discovered that when you assign such an essay topic, you tend to get essays not really about the poem, but about God and religion more generally. Similarly, a colleague of mine reports that her practice is to ask her students to pretend that they are about to adapt the poem into a modern film and to cast famous actors in the key roles. Here, again, a relatively simple exercise can have profoundly surprising results which often lead to discussions about gender, race, politics and religion far beyond the immediate context of the poem. Deciding, for example, which famous Hollywood starlet should play Eve is not as frivolous as it initially sounds – it essentially forces the students to engage very early on with their own prejudices when coming to analyse such an archetypical female character. Such is the unique power of *Paradise Lost*. Despite its apparent remoteness and baroque grandeur, it speaks to us today about some of our deepest and most fundamental human concerns, and students usually respond to this instinctively and in many cases viscerally. The teacher's task should always be, therefore, to engage the debate in the Miltonic spirit and keep it going, always referring to key passages of the text for close reading to complicate perspectives and challenge students to argue and make adjustments to their claims. From this initial confrontation with the poem's 'great argument' everything else should follow, whether the teacher wants to focus more on questions of style and poetics, or historical context and politics.

Before considering some possible course templates, there are a few basic approaches which should prove useful in any given scenario, whether the poem is taught in its entirety in a course devoted entirely to Milton or only in brief highlights in longer cultural and literary surveys. The following are some helpful ground rules.

Text and context

Text should always take precedent over context. *Paradise Lost* is a rich poem opening up to numerous important contexts, but focusing too much on these without anchoring such discussions in actual passages from the poem can soon drown out the art of the poem in contextual detail and alienate students. While many teachers feel that it is prudent to give a number of introductory lectures setting up the historical, political, theological and philosophical contexts before reading the poem, such an approach is not always effective because students will then find it difficult to relate such general lectures to the poem. It is always preferable to address each of these contexts as they emerge from the poem itself in the process of close readings.

For example, historical questions about Milton's republicanism can be brought into discussion when analysing Satan's opening speeches, theological questions when addressing the council in heaven between the Father and the Son in Book III, and so on. Where the teacher feels some initial background of the period is nevertheless essential, it is possible to assign background reading of one or more of the essays in one of the Milton handbooks and companions (see bibliography), or even to give a short research assignment related to a good introductory text. A still excellent text to use in such cases is Graham Parry's *The Seventeenth Century: The Intellectual and Cultural Context of English Literature, 1603–1700* (Longman: London and New York, 1989).

Getting to grips with the argument

Because the structure of *Paradise Lost* is carefully considered, it is best to trust Milton's plan when reading the poem in its entirety and not disrupt this structure by having students read later books first. Milton wanted his readers to start with hell and Satan and that is always the best place to start. A good way into the poem's elusive didactic engagement with its intended 'fit' readers is then to alert students straightaway to the function of voice in the poem. Who is the narrator? Is he omniscient and reliable or perhaps a partisan character? What sort of claims to authority does he make? As reading in the poem progresses, can we say it is the same narrator throughout? Does he change? What sort of interpretative and ethical demands does he make of us? Are there other authority figures and voices of instruction in the poem? These sorts of questions are important because they focus the students' attention on their own active role as readers and disabuse them of the illusion that *Paradise Lost* offers a predetermined and self-explanatory didactic message imposed on a familiar biblical narrative. The quicker the students get a sense of the poem's competing layers of authority and interpretation the more enjoyment they will get from the sense of responsibility conferred on them as readers.

Annotated editions

A big obstacle for students coming to the poem for the first time is Milton's ostentatious learning and seeming pedantry. Many students skim the text, often not stopping to check the story behind this or that obscure mythological name or biblical reference. Having students use a good annotated edition of the poem is therefore crucial. The single poem editions outlined in the annotated bibliography in the next chapter in this *Guide* are the most suitable and reliable (consult the bibliography for details about each of these).

> When reading the poem with students, always encourage them to dwell on the many mythological and biblical proper names and allusions. It is also a good idea, if possible, to give substance to such demands by giving students a written assignment asking them to research a set of allusions and write about their significance in a given passage.

Milton's English and questions of style

Another potential obstacle for first-time readers and students is coming to terms with the complexities of Milton's style and idiom. Here, doing close reading of particularly difficult passages becomes essential. Do not waste time by giving elaborate lectures about rhetoric or syntax above the text, but have students analyse syntactically one of Satan's or God's speeches and discuss its rhetorical effect in class with them. Alert students to the importance also of single words in the poem, encouraging them to make a list, while reading the poem, of puns, thematic words and other stylistic effects which occur to them.

> I have found from experience that giving a short dictionary assignment at an early stage of a Milton course can also go a very long way towards easing students into the habit of not taking Milton's English for granted. Today, the complete *Oxford English Dictionary* is available as an electronic resource in most universities. Simply assign students a suitable passage from the poem and ask them to check words in the *OED*, noting the many possible uses of a given word that would have been current in Milton's time. Then ask them to analyse the passage for its literary and stylistic effect based solely on the place of a given word in a line. Students who do this once might well begin to do this as a matter of practice when asked to submit longer work of their own later on.

Teaching *Paradise Lost* in a course or seminar devoted entirely to the poem or to Milton's poetic works more generally

The most natural way to teach *Paradise Lost* is in an advanced undergraduate or graduate course devoted solely to the poem or to Milton's poetic *oeuvre* in general. Academic terms vary in length from country to country, but in the majority of cases, assuming the course in question is not annual, a teacher should have anything between eight and twenty-four meetings to work with the material. If there is time, there is no substitute for reading *Paradise Lost* in its entirety, book by book, assigning one or two books per meeting for close discussion and analysis. In courses of this nature, where the poem can be read at leisure, there is ample time to pay close attention to Milton's poetic artistry and analyse at length key passages and speeches for their rhetorical and stylistic effects. By tying these effects to the question of reading and interpretation and the sorts of reactions such effects elicit from the reader, students can begin appreciating the detail and intricacy of the poem. If *Paradise Lost* is taught alongside other poetic and perhaps prose works of Milton in an overview of his *oeuvre* then the teacher has to situate the poem within the context of the larger Miltonic canon. This can be achieved in a number of ways, either by taking a biographical-chronological approach, or a thematic-conceptual one. The benefit of a chronological approach is that it allows the teacher to focus on Milton's creative development and address important questions that emerge from such a perspective, for example on the formation and projection of Milton's poetic persona throughout his work, or on his self-conscious exploration of different genres and different poetic styles in different periods in his life. Conversely, the benefit of the thematic-conceptual approach is that it allows the teacher to focus more directly on key ideas and themes which run as a thread throughout the Miltonic corpus. Such an ambitious syllabus is more difficult to construct, but it can be very rewarding potentially for both students and teachers.

For example, a teacher might begin by tracing the themes of tyranny and liberty from Milton's early poetry and 'Lycidas', through *Paradise Lost* and the political sonnets, all the way to *Samson Agonistes*. It is possible to plot similar outlines for themes related to generic experimentation and poetic influence, the use and imitation of the classics, Milton's projection of his authority and persona, ideas of monism and materialist philosophy, various theological topics, and of course important political concerns such as radicalism, puritanism and republicanism. As the thematic strands begin to accumulate, the teacher can then draw connections between them, resulting in a deeper thematic understanding of the Miltonic *oeuvre* than is possible with a more straightforward chronological approach. In each case, however, the same principle outlined above of direct engagement with the poem's argument should apply, never neglecting even in the discussions of thematics questions of voice, rhetoric and style.

Teaching aids and essential reading

For *Paradise Lost* itself, any teaching aid which can enhance the students' sense of the poem's musicality and vibrant imagery is always a bonus. *Paradise Lost* has inspired a great deal of art and bringing to classes famous illustrations of the poem, for example by John Baptist Medina, Gustave Doré, William Blake and even images from contemporary pop culture and comic art, can be a good way to discuss the poem's unique visual-imaginative dimension. This approach is especially useful when trying to tease out the iconographic elements Milton brings into play in the poem (for more on this aspect of the poem consult works by R. Frye and D. McColley listed in the bibliography). *Paradise Lost*, however, primarily works on sound. It is a good idea to have students read passages aloud in class so they can get a feel for the tone and rhythm of the poetry. Reading aloud, especially speeches spoken by characters such as Satan, God or Eve, is a good way to help students get the sense of character which emerges from the prosody, tone and syntactical rhythms of a given passage. For example, just by having two different students read aloud parts of the heavenly council in Book III, or one of Satan's stirring speeches from Books I–II, it is possible to explore the logical and emotional ambivalence of the language attached to hell or heaven respectively.

In terms of essential reading, opinions vary as to how much criticism undergraduates should be made responsible for, and it is certainly better to have them first come to terms with the poem in its own right before looking at other critics and scholars. Where students are used to doing more independent research, it might be useful to assign some reading of one or more of the introductory essays to be found in the various Milton handbooks and companions (see bibliography). For more advanced courses, where some engagement with critics is requisite, I recommend starting off with the items highlighted with an asterisk (*) in the main bibliography list in this *Guide*.

A typical criticism assignment might be to read Lewis, Empson and Fish (see bibliography) and write a response relating to the justice of Milton's God, or perhaps to set up a debate in class between so-called 'satanic' critics (Blake, Empson, Forsyth and possibly Pullman as well) and exponents of more traditional readings (for example Lewis, Burden and Danielson). Alternatively, if style and form is the focus, it is always a good idea to have students re-engage with the groundbreaking criticism of Christopher Ricks and the so-called 'Milton controversy' of the early twentieth century as a way into a discussion of the poem's major stylistic features and effects.

Teaching *Paradise Lost* as a component in a wider period course alongside other contemporary poets and authors

It is not always possible to read *Paradise Lost* in class in its entirety, and many lecturers working on the early modern period often find they have to incorporate a few lectures on the poem into larger period survey courses. Apart from obviously insisting that students read the poem in its entirety ahead of these lectures, the teacher in these cases nevertheless faces a difficult task in selecting the points on which to focus. Theoretically, it is possible to deliver only a single lecture on *Paradise Lost*, but such a lecture will be inevitably reductive. To do justice to the poem, a minimum of three separate lectures are required, and how these get set up depends to a great extent on the survey course in question. Historical surveys will naturally wish to situate *Paradise Lost* politically as a subversive Restoration poem, drawing chiefly and quickly on the poem's main political argument about liberty, right reason and tyranny. If the focus is more on the literary continuum from Milton's Elizabethan predecessors to his Restoration contemporaries, then obviously more should be said about the place of the poem in the English epic tradition, its creative indebtedness to Spenser and Shakespeare, and its subversive dialogue with Restoration literary culture and such poets as Marvell and Dryden (noting, for example, Milton's defence of blank verse appended to the 1668 edition of the poem, Marvell's dedicatory poem to *Paradise Lost*, and Dryden's efforts to turn *Paradise Lost* into an opera). Whichever context the teacher is leaning towards, it is best to then divide the poem as I do in the commentary section of this *Guide* into hell, heaven and paradise, and to allocate however many classes can be set aside for *Paradise Lost* to each of these sections in equal measure. A thematic and stylistic overview of each section should then be complemented ideally with the close reading of select passages and class discussions over the main themes which anchor the poem into the survey course in question.

Teaching aids and essential reading

Naturally, when spending as little as three lectures on *Paradise Lost* in an introductory survey course there is no place for bothering students with criticism, though again one or two introductory essays from one of the Milton handbooks can be assigned as further reading where the teacher feels students will need to supplement the lectures with more comprehensive contextual detail.

Teaching *Paradise Lost* against the specific historical background of seventeenth-century politics and radicalism

Milton scholars for a long time now have been engaging in the process of historicising Milton's poetry while emphasising its complex engagement with contemporary political debates about liberty and tyranny in the domestic, religious, and public spheres of English life in the seventeenth century. Where before the 1980s *Paradise Lost* largely stood apart from, and above, Milton's profuse polemical prose, a common practice today in many academic circles is to contextualise the poem in light of Milton's political writings, and to see both bodies of work as extensions of the same intellectual endeavour to shape and reform the English church and state. In particular, such an approach has the merit of bringing *Paradise Lost* into contemporary focus as a poem which can stimulate students to re-engage with important political questions about civic responsibility, free speech, toleration and nonconformity, and the formation of national identities. Teachers who wish to focus on this growing trend in Milton scholarship might well wish to tailor a seminar or course specifically centred on this approach. Such a seminar will naturally involve wide reading in Milton's prose alongside a comparative thematic and generic consideration of *Paradise Lost*. For longer courses it is also possible to include Milton's political sonnets as well, and the two later major poems of *Paradise Regained* and *Samson Agonistes*. In courses where the main focus is *Paradise Lost*, however, there are several central questions which should always shape such a syllabus. As discussed in the historical-political context sections of the commentary in this *Guide*, Milton does not posit absolute political ideas in the poem, but submits them to debate as contested ideas against a set of abstract ideological beliefs about the nature of true liberty.

A key recommended approach in this context is to try and work out with the students what the concept of 'true liberty' actually meant to Milton in different stages of his life and political thinking. This question should then easily open up into numerous other areas of inquiry, including Milton's emerging republicanism, his views on war and militarisation, his concept of civil duty and responsibility, the extent of his agreement with radical sectarians and the political aspirations of puritans, and so on. Again, even in a course of this nature, *Paradise Lost* should remain at the centre of inquiry and teachers should take care not to lose sight of the fact that *Paradise Lost* is not a prose treatise, but a richly complex and allusive poem engaging creatively with political questions and ideas.

Teaching aids and essential reading

A course of this nature will require a great deal of historical contextualisation. Rather than submitting students to dry lectures, it is again best to discuss the various historical-political questions and contexts as they arise from the texts being read in class. Milton's prose fills up eight massive volumes in the definitive Yale edition of his *Complete Prose* and to expect students to read all of it over one course is impractical. The prose treatises which are most relevant to a political discussion of *Paradise Lost* and which would fit well together on one syllabus are *Areopagitica* (1644), *Of Education* (1644), *The Doctrine and Discipline of Divorce* (1644), *The Tenure of Kings and Magistrates* (1649), and *The Ready and Easy Way to Establish a Free Commonwealth* (1660). These can then be supplemented, where relevant, with shorter excerpts from other treatises, especially from *The Reason of Church-Government* (1642), the Latin defences of the English people written during the Protectorate, or Milton's *History of Britain* (1670). Also, if the teacher is throwing a wider net on political writings in the period in an attempt to situate Milton among these, then of course passages from the writings of other political thinkers in the period, including and especially perhaps Thomas Hobbes's *Leviathan*, could be brought in as well for contrast.

Essential critical reading in a course like this should include essays and chapters from books representing major landmarks in the historicist study of Milton. From the annotated bibliography provided in this *Guide* entries of essays and chapters from books by Achinstein, Bennet, Coffey, Dzelzainis, Knoppers, Loewenstein, Mueller, and Norbrook should form the core of any reading list, supplemented with introductory essays from the respective Milton handbooks. Among these, Dzelzainis's contributions to the *Cambridge Companion* and the *Oxford Handbook* are especially useful, as are the essays by Brown, Keeble, Rumrich, Hadfield and Raymond in the Blackwell *Companion* (see bibliography). For a more general background, students might also find very useful some of the essays contained in N. H. Keeble (ed.), *The Cambridge Companion to Writing of the English Revolution* (Cambridge: Cambridge University Press, 2001) and in Graham Parry and Joad Raymond (eds), *Milton and the Terms of Liberty* (Woodbridge: D. S. Brewer, 2002).

Teaching *Paradise Lost* in relation to the greater epic tradition of European literature

Paradise Lost is not just the greatest epic poem ever written in the English language, it is also one of the greatest epic poems in the wider European tradition. At the outset of the poem, the narrator declares that what we are about to read pursues 'Things unattempted yet in prose or rhyme' (I. 16). This line, echoing similar words in Ariosto's epic romance *Orlando Furioso*, lays claim to originality and novelty but in its very nature as a quotation it also alludes to the poem's deep awareness of the literary tradition with which it competes. Because Milton actively and creatively competes in his poem with his great predecessors Homer and Virgil, and closer to home with Spenser as well, a good way to teach the poem in terms of its generic and literary complexity is to situate it in a literary epic tradition. There are several different groupings *Paradise Lost* can be placed in. Where the teacher possesses adequate training in the classics, a wonderful option is to teach a course on epic poetry in the European tradition with a syllabus covering Homer's *Iliad*, Virgil's *Aeneid*, Dante's *Commedia*, one or two medieval romances, culminating with a study of the English tradition inaugurated by Chaucer, Spenser and finally Milton's *Paradise Lost*. For longer courses with more ambitious scope, it is possible to include in such a syllabus Homer's *Odyssey*, Apollonius of Rhodes' *Argonautika*, and crucially perhaps Ovid's *Metamorphoses* as well, ending with the modern masterpiece of Derek Walcott's Nobel Prize winning poem *Omeros*. Alternatively, it is possible to focus more narrowly on the English tradition to include a syllabus that covers *Beowulf*, *The Canterbury Tales*, *The Faerie Queene*, *Paradise Lost*, Dryden's translation of the *Aeneid*, Pope's *Dunciad*, Wordsworth's *The Prelude*, and again possibly ending with Walcott's *Omeros* (though it makes little sense to study Walcott's poem without some consideration of classical epic as well). Situating *Paradise Lost* in this way into a wider syllabus addressing a long literary tradition makes it possible to study in a more precise and detailed manner the generic subtlety and inventiveness of Milton's epic.

When tying the various texts of such a syllabus together it is possible to focus on a number of leading questions or topics other than thematic considerations of content. Key leading questions might include an examination of the respective functions of the epic narrators, narrative time schemes and structure, epic similes and other common literary devices, prosody and rhyme, and questions relating to literary influence, allusion, and imitation across the texts selected.

Teaching aids and essential reading

With respect to teaching aids for *Paradise Lost*, the same materials listed above should be used, though in this case it is arguably a good idea to have students look at Milton's Trinity Manuscript drafts of *Paradise Lost* as well to gain a sense of the poem's creative development. Transcriptions of the manuscript draft are available in most annotated editions of the poem, in some source books and in a facsimile reprint, *John Milton Poems: Reproduced in Facsimile from the Manuscript in Trinity College, Cambridge, with a Transcript*, ed. W. A. Wright (Menston, Ilkley: Scolar Press, 1970). In terms of reading relating specifically to *Paradise Lost*, the following entries from the annotated bibliography in this *Guide* are the most relevant to a syllabus of this nature: Burrow, Creaser, Ferry, Forsyth, Frye (Roland), Hale, Lewalski, Lewis, Martindale, Quint, Rajan, Ricks, Teskey, Triep and Webber. Another two studies which would be very useful in this context are Thomas M. Greene's *The Descent from Heaven: A Study in Epic Continuity* (New Haven, CT: Yale University Press, 1963) and the same author's *The Light in Troy: Imitation and Discovery in Renaissance Poetry* (New Haven, CT: Yale University Press, 1982).

Bibliography

This chapter contains a partly annotated bibliography of select works on Milton which students and teachers might find useful. A comprehensive bibliography citing all available criticism on *Paradise Lost* would be impractical as it would likely take up as many pages as this *Guide*. Students who wish to delve deeper and wider into Milton scholarship can easily do so by following up the many notes and bibliographies contained in the studies mentioned below. Entries in all sections are arranged in alphabetical order according to surname.

Editions of the poem

The text of *Paradise Lost* invariably used today by readers is the revised text of the 1674 edition of the poem, divided into twelve books and containing Milton's arguments and prefatory materials. Some modern editors modernise the spelling, standardise the use of capitalisation and elisions, and amend in very few cases variants based on the earlier 1667 edition of the poem. The text of the poem itself is not under copyright law and is widely available on the Internet in various html forms. The best and most accessible version of the poem on the Internet is the lightly annotated and easy to use version to be found on Dartmouth College's website, *The Milton Reading Room*, edited by Thomas H. Luxon:

url: http://www.dartmouth.edu/~milton/reading_room/contents/index.shtml

For annotated single editions of the poem, today's reader has many options to choose from but the most scholarly, sound and widely available are the following (listed alphabetically by editor):

John Milton: Paradise Lost, ed. Roy Flannagan (New York: Macmillan, 1993).

An old spelling, annotated edition with a helpful introduction and good, informative notes accompanying the text on each page. It is also distinguished by its emphasis on the encounter between the poem and modern literary theory. Now more easily accessed in the complete one-volume *Riverside Milton* edited by Flannagan, this edition is in many respects eclipsed by the Fowler edition below. However, if readers and teachers wish to use an old spelling edition, this is the one to choose.

Milton: Paradise Lost, ed. Alastair Fowler, 2nd edn, Longman Annotated English Poets series (London and New York: Longman, 1998).
By far the most detailed and comprehensively annotated modernised edition of the poem (Fowler modernises spelling but not punctuation), more suitable perhaps for graduate rather than undergraduate students. Some readers might find the dense notes cramming each page distracting, but this remains, as one review put it, a very Bible of Milton. This edition is also very useful in pointing to relevant criticism about key passages in the poem up to 1998.

John Milton: Paradise Lost, ed. John Leonard, Penguin Classics (London: Penguin, 2000). Also available as a separate entry in *John Milton: The Complete Poems*, ed. John Leonard (London: Penguin, 1998).
The edition used in this *Guide*. It is distinguished by its lighter approach to modernisation. It retains many of the elisions and original spellings of the 1674 edition, where these are justified metrically. Leonard's notes are less intrusive and more economical than Flannagan's or Fowler's, necessarily providing therefore much less information, but they stand out for their special emphasis on the peculiar flexibility of Milton's language.

John Milton: The Major Works including Paradise Lost, ed. Stephen Orgel and Jonathan Goldberg, Oxford World's Classics (Oxford: Oxford University Press, 1991).
Contains an accessible and very lightly annotated modernised edition of the poem alongside all of Milton's minor as well as major poetry and select prose (which is a significant bonus). The notes are not as useful as in the editions listed above, but this is still a worthy scholarly replacement for these. A good edition to use in courses surveying *Paradise Lost* alongside Milton's other major poems and prose works.

Companions and handbooks

The year 2008 saw the celebration of the 400th anniversary of Milton's birth, leading to a proliferation in new companions and handbooks to his work meant to update and replace older editions and handbooks from previous decades. The various available handbooks and introductory guides to Milton's life and work offer first-time readers and students the best initial access to a very dense field of scholarship. There is much to choose from here, and many of these handbooks overlap in the material and insights they offer.

The following is just a short sample of the most widely available and useful ones for students and teachers:

Corns, Thomas N. (ed.), *A Companion to Milton* (Oxford: Blackwell, 2001, 2003).
A comprehensive and detailed companion offering a range of essays placing Milton's life and work in a wide set of historical and literary contexts. Its five separate introductory essays on *Paradise Lost* together offer an excellent overall introduction to the poem.

Danielson, Dennis (ed.), *The Cambridge Companion to Milton*, 2nd edn (Cambridge: Cambridge University Press, 1999).
Now quite dated by comparison with newer companions, it still offers important and insightful introductory essays on *Paradise Lost* students might find very useful, most notably by John Carey on Satan, Barbara Lewalski on genre, John Leonard on language and Dennis Danielson on theology.

Dobranski, Stephen B. (ed.), *Milton in Context* (Cambridge: Cambridge University Press, 2010).
A very useful and informative handbook which takes context as its primary focus. A range of short, illuminating essays contextualise almost every conceivable aspect of Milton's work, from his composition process and various experiments in different poetic genres to a range of historical and cultural topics. It is the only companion which contains truly valuable introductory essays on such important Miltonic topics as astronomy, education, music and the New World, among others.

McDowell, Nicholas and Nigel Smith (eds), *The Oxford Handbook of Milton* (Oxford: Oxford University Press, 2009).
Similar in scope and depth to the Blackwell *Companion* listed above, the more recent *Oxford Handbook* takes a slightly different organisational approach to its essays, focusing in greater detail on the range of Milton's prose and poetic works. It offers a total of eight introductory essays on *Paradise Lost*, some of which, like the essay on the prosody of the poem by John Creaser, represent truly new and important work. In its range of emphases the *Oxford Handbook* best represents current trends in Milton studies.

Chronologies and biographies

Unlike Shakespeare, for example, about whose life little is known with any certainty, Milton's relatively long life is an open book. This also means there is a lot of it. Milton biographies tend to be very long and unwieldy simply because they have to cover vast amounts of available material. Most editions of Milton's poetry and the various companions mentioned above contain shorter, more accessible chronologies and biographical sketches, but these inevitably omit much. Gordon Campbell's *A Milton Chronology* (Basingstoke: Macmillan, 1997) offers in this respect a more accessible chronological account of Milton's life and works, but if readers want to get a deeper sense of the poet and his life there is no way to avoid the major scholarly biographies on offer:

Campbell, Gordon and Thomas N. Corns, *John Milton: Life, Work, and Thought* (Oxford: Oxford University Press, 2008).
> The most recent biography is also arguably the most user-friendly and balanced of the group. It offers fresh archival evidence and new interpretations of the available material, and places Milton's works in the wider historical, cultural, social and intellectual contexts of his time.

Darbishire, Helen (ed.), *The Early Lives of Milton* (London: Constable, 1932).
> Still the only available modern edition which collects all of the early biographies of Milton written within a few years and decades of the poet's death. Many of the modern biographies depend on the material contained in these early accounts and readers might well benefit from glancing at these in their pristine form. Readers should also be aware, however, that much in these early accounts is open to considerable debate and interpretation.

Hill, Christopher, *Milton and the English Revolution* (London: Faber and Faber, 1977).
> When eminent historian Christopher Hill, famous for his groundbreaking work on the English Civil War, turned to write a biography of Milton he astounded with the rich contextual detail into which he cast Milton's major prose and poetry. Hill's interpretations and conclusions have not gone unchallenged, but few biographies of Milton since have given such an informed account of the period in which Milton wrote, and of the likely ideological forces which engaged his thought. Hill's historical biography is also by far the most gripping and readable.

Lewalski, Barbara K., *The Life of John Milton: A Critical Biography* (Oxford: Blackwell, 2000).
> A rather dense critical biography of Milton which gives a detailed account of the poet's life through a chronological and literary assessment of his works. Biographically it is mostly derivative, but it also contains very useful analytical overviews of Milton's poetry and prose, as well as of major trends in Milton criticism.

Parker, William Riley [1968], *Milton: A Biography*, 2 vols, 2nd edn, ed. Gordon Campbell (Oxford: Clarendon Press, 1996).
  For decades the definitive biography of Milton. Its massive two volumes contain all of the available material any reader is ever likely to want to know about Milton's life. More recent biographies have refined perspectives, and in some cases unearthed new archival evidence that sheds new light on this material, but Parker's biography remains the definitive work. Its unwieldy two-volume format, however, makes it the least accessible of the available Milton biographies.

Major single-author studies on or relating to *Paradise Lost*

Over the decades some studies of *Paradise Lost*, whether book-length monographs or shorter articles in journals and edited volumes, have stood above the rest for their singularity of voice and overall contribution to the field. The following is a list of the most important studies which any student of Milton wanting to gain a purchase on the available scholarship on *Paradise Lost* should eventually be familiar with. The variety of approaches and methodologies on offer here is vast, testifying to the many different theoretical perspectives Milton's poetry lends itself to. The best of these studies, however, transcend simplistic theoretical labels and engage with the poem on its own complex terms. Entries marked with an asterisk (*) indicate canonical titles which should form the basis of any course bibliography and are essential first reading for students wishing to familiarise themselves with major debates in Milton criticism.

* Achinstein, Sharon, *Milton and the Revolutionary Reader* (Princeton: Princeton University Press, 1994).
Achinstein, Sharon, 'Toleration in Milton's Epics: A Chimera?', in Sharon Achinstein and Elizabeth Sauer (eds), *Milton and Toleration* (Oxford: Oxford University Press, 2007), pp. 224–42.
Belsey, Catherine, *John Milton: Language, Gender, Power* (Oxford: Blackwell, 1988).
* Bennet, Joan S., 'God, Satan, and King Charles: Milton's Royal Portraits', *PMLA*, 92 (May 1977), 441–57.
Bennet, Joan S., *Reviving Liberty: Radical Christian Humanism in Milton's Great Poems* (Cambridge, MA, and London: Harvard University Press, 1989).
Broadbent, J. B., *Some Graver Subject: An Essay on* Paradise Lost (London: Chatto and Windus, 1960).
Budick, Sanford, *The Dividing Muse: Images of Disjunction in Milton's Poetry* (New Haven, CT, and London: Yale University Press, 1985).
Burden, Dennis H., *The Logical Epic: A Study of the Argument of* Paradise Lost (London: Routledge and Kegan Paul, 1967).

Burrow, Colin, *Epic Romance: Homer to Milton* (Oxford: Clarendon Press, 1993).

Christopher, Georgia B., *Milton and the Science of the Saints* (Princeton: Princeton University Press, 1982).

Coffey, John, 'Pacifist, Quietist, or Patient Militant? John Milton and the Restoration', *Milton Studies*, 42 (2002), 149–74.

* Corns, Thomas N., *Milton's Language* (Oxford: Blackwell, 1990).

* Corns, Thomas N., *Regaining* Paradise Lost (London and New York: Longman, 1994).

* Creaser, John, '"Service is Perfect Freedom": Paradox and Prosodic Style in *Paradise Lost*', *Review of English Studies*, 53 (2007), 268–315.

* Danielson, Dennis R., *Milton's Good God: A Study in Literary Theodicy* (Cambridge and New York: Cambridge University Press, 1982).

Diekhoff, John S., *Milton's* Paradise Lost: *A Commentary on the Argument* (New York: Humanities Press, 1963).

Dzelzainis, Martin, 'Milton's Classical Republicanism', in David Armitage, Armand Himy and Quentin Skinner (eds), *Milton and Republicanism* (Cambridge: Cambridge University Press, 1995), pp. 3–24.

Dzelzainis, Martin, 'Milton and Antitrinitarianism', in Sharon Achinstein and Elizabeth Sauer (eds), *Milton and Toleration* (Oxford: Oxford University Press, 2007), pp. 171–85.

Edwards, Karen L., *Milton and the Natural World: Science and Poetry in* Paradise Lost (Cambridge: Cambridge University Press, 1999).

* Empson, William [1961], *Milton's God*, revised edn (London: Chatto and Windus, 1965).

Evans, J. Martin, Paradise Lost *and the Genesis Tradition* (Oxford: Clarendon Press, 1968).

* Fallon, Stephen M., *Milton among the Philosophers: Poetry and Materialism in Seventeenth-Century England* (Ithaca, NY, and London: Cornell University Press, 1991).

Fallon, Stephen M., *Milton's Peculiar Grace: Self-Representation and Authority* (Ithaca, NY, and London: Cornell University Press, 2007).

* Ferry, Anne, *Milton's Epic Voice: The Narrator in* Paradise Lost (Cambridge, MA: Harvard University Press, 1963).

* Fish, Stanley E. [1967], *Surprised by Sin: The Reader in* Paradise Lost, 2nd edn (London: Macmillan, 1997).

* Forsyth, Neil, *The Satanic Epic* (Princeton: Princeton University Press, 2003).

Frye, Northrop, *Five Essays on Milton's Epics* (London: Routledge and Kegan Paul, 1966).

* Frye, Roland Mushat, *Milton's Imagery and the Visual Arts: Iconographic Tradition in the Epic Poems* (Princeton: Princeton University Press, 1978).

Grossman, Marshall, *'Authors to Themselves': Milton and the Revelation of History* (Cambridge: Cambridge University Press, 1987).

Grossman, Marshall, 'The Genders of God and the Redemption of the Flesh in *Paradise Lost*', in Catherine Gimelli Martin (ed.), *Milton and Gender* (Cambridge: Cambridge University Press, 2004), pp. 95–114.

Hale, John K., *Milton's Languages: The Impact of Multilingualism on Style* (Cambridge: Cambridge University Press, 1997).

Haskin, Dayton, *Milton's Burden of Interpretation* (Philadelphia: Pennsylvania University Press, 1994).

* Kermode, Frank, 'Adam Unparadised', in Frank Kermode (ed.), *The Living Milton: Essays by Various Hands* (London: Routledge, 1960), pp. 85–123.

Kerrigan, William, *The Prophetic Milton* (Charlottesville: Virginia University Press, 1974).

Kerrigan, William, *The Sacred Complex: On the Psychogenesis of* Paradise Lost (Cambridge, MA, and London: Harvard University Press, 1983).

Kerrigan, William and Gordon Braden. 'Milton's Coy Eve: *Paradise Lost* and Renaissance Love Poetry', *ELH*, 53 (1986), 27–51.

Kolbrener, William, *Milton's Warring Angels: A Study of Critical Engagements* (Cambridge: Cambridge University Press, 1997).

Knoppers, Laura Lunger, *Historicizing Milton: Spectacle, Power, and Poetry in Restoration England* (Athens and London: Georgia University Press, 1994).

Labriola, Albert C., '"Thy Humiliation Shall Exalt": The Christology of *Paradise Lost*', *Milton Studies*, 15 (1981), 29–42.

* Leonard, John, *Naming in Paradise: Milton and the Language of Adam and Eve* (Oxford: Clarendon Press, 1990).

Leonard, John, 'Milton, Lucretius, and "the void profound of unessential Night"', in Kirstin A. Pruitt and Charles W. Durham (eds), *Living Texts: Interpreting Milton* (Selinsgrove, PA, and London: Susquehanna University Press, 2000), pp. 198–217.

* Lewalski, Barbara K., Paradise Lost *and the Rhetoric of Literary Forms* (Princeton: Princeton University Press, 1985).

* Lewis, C. S., *A Preface to* Paradise Lost (London: Oxford University Press, 1942).

Lieb, Michael, *Poetics of the Holy: A Reading of* Paradise Lost (Chapel Hill: North Carolina University Press, 1981).

Lieb, Michael, *Theological Milton: Deity, Discourse and Heresy in the Miltonic Canon* (Pittsburgh: Duquesne University Press, 2007).

Loewenstein, David, *Milton and the Drama of History: Historical Vision, Iconoclasm, and the Literary Imagination* (Cambridge: Cambridge University Press, 1990).

Loewenstein, David, *Representing Revolution in Milton and his Contemporaries: Religion, Politics, and Polemics in Radical Puritanism* (Cambridge: Cambridge University Press, 2001).

Luxon, Thomas H., *Single Imperfection: Milton, Marriage and Friendship* (Pittsburgh: Duquesne University Press, 2005).

MacCallum, Hugh R., *Milton and the Sons of God: The Divine Image in Milton's Epic Poetry* (Toronto: University of Toronto Press, 1986).

* McColley, Diane Kelsey, *Milton's Eve* (Urbana, IL, and London: University of Illinois Press, 1983).

McColley, Diane Kelsey, *A Gust for Paradise: Milton's Eden and the Visual Arts* (Urbana, IL, and London: University of Illinois Press, 1993).

Madsen, William G., *From Shadowy Types to Truth: Studies in Milton's Symbolism* (New Haven, CT, and London: Yale University Press, 1968).

Martin, Catherine Gimelli, *The Ruins of Allegory*: Paradise Lost *and the Metamorphosis of Epic Convention* (Durham, NC, and London: Duke University Press, 1998).

* Martindale, Charles, *John Milton and the Transformation of Ancient Epic* (London: Croom Helm, 1986).

Martz, Louis L., *Poet of Exile: A Study in Milton's Poetry* (New Haven, CT, and London: Yale University Press, 1980).

Morrison, Sarah R., 'When Worlds Collide: The Central Naturalistic Narrative and the Allegorical Dimension to *Paradise Lost*', in Kirstin A. Pruitt and Charles W. Durham (eds), *Living Texts: Interpreting Milton* (Selinsgrove, PA, and London: Susquehanna University Press, 2000), pp. 178–97.

Mueller, Janel, 'Contextualizing Milton's Nascent Republicanism', in Paul Stanwood (ed.), *Of Poetry and Politics: New Essays on Milton and His World* (Binghamton, NY: Medieval and Renaissance Texts and Studies, 1995), pp. 263–82.

Norbrook, David, *Writing the English Republic: Poetry, Rhetoric, Politics, 1627–1660* (Cambridge: Cambridge University Press, 1999).

Nuttall, A. D., *The Alternative Trinity: Gnostic Heresy in Marlowe, Milton, and Blake* (Oxford: Clarendon Press, 1998).

Nyquist, Mary, 'The Genesis of Gendered Subjectivity in the Divorce Tracts and in *Paradise Lost*', in Mary Nyquist and Margaret W. Ferguson (eds), *Re-membering Milton: Essays on the Texts and Traditions* (New York: Methuen, 1987), pp. 99–127.

Patterson, Annabel, *Milton's Words* (Oxford: Oxford University Press, 2009).

Picciotto, Joanna, 'Reforming the Garden: The Experimentalist Eden and *Paradise Lost*', *ELH*, 72.1 (2005), 23–78.

* Poole, William, *Milton and the Idea of the Fall* (Cambridge: Cambridge University Press, 2005).

Quint, David, *Epic and Empire: Politics and Generic Form from Virgil to Milton* (Princeton: Princeton University Press, 1993).

Quint, David, 'Fear of Falling: Icarus, Phaethon, and Lucretius in *Paradise Lost*', *Renaissance Quarterly*, 57.3 (2004), 315–45.

Radzinowicz, Mary Ann, *Milton's Epics and the Book of Psalms* (Princeton: Princeton University Press, 1989).

* Rajan, Balachandra, '*Paradise Lost*: The Uncertain Epic', *Milton Studies*, 17 (1983), 105–19.

Rajan, Balachandra, *Milton and the Climates of Reading: Essays by Balachandra Rajan*, ed. Elizabeth Sauer (Toronto: University of Toronto Press, 2007).

Revard, Stella, *The War in Heaven*: Paradise Lost *and the Tradition of Satan's Rebellion* (Ithaca, NY: Cornell University Press, 1980).

* Ricks, Christopher, *Milton's Grand Style* (Oxford: Clarendon Press, 1963).

Rogers, John, *The Matter of Revolution: Science, Poetry, and Politics in the Age of Milton* (Ithaca, NY: Cornell University Press, 1996).

Rogers, John, 'Transported Touch: the Fruit of Marriage in *Paradise Lost*', in Catherine Gimelli Martin (ed.), *Milton and Gender* (Cambridge: Cambridge University Press, 2004), pp. 115–32.

Rosenblatt, Jason P., *Torah and Law in* Paradise Lost (Princeton: Princeton University Press, 1994).

* Rumrich, John Peter, *Milton Unbound: Controversy and Interpretation* (Cambridge: Cambridge University Press, 1996).

Rumrich, John Peter, 'Milton's Arianism: Why it Matters', in Stephen B. Dobranski and John P. Rumrich (eds), *Milton and Heresy* (Cambridge: Cambridge University Press, 1998), pp. 75–92.

Samuel, Irene, 'The Dialogue in Heaven: A Reconsideration of *Paradise Lost* III, 1-417', *PMLA*, 72.4 (1957), 601–11.

Sauer, Elizabeth, *Barbarous Dissonance and Images of Voice in Milton's Epics* (Montreal and Kingston: McGill-Queen's University Press, 1996).

Schwartz, Regina, *Remembering and Repeating: On Milton's Theology and Poetics* (Chicago and London: Chicago University Press, 1988, 1993).

Shawcross, John T., *John Milton: The Self and the World* (Lexington, KY: Kentucky University Press, 1993).

Silver, Victoria, *Imperfect Sense: The Predicament of Milton's Irony* (Princeton: Princeton University Press, 2001).

Stein, Arnold S., *Answerable Style: Essays on* Paradise Lost (Minneapolis: Minnesota University Press, 1967).

Stevens, Paul, *Imagination and the Presence of Shakespeare in* Paradise Lost (Madison: Wisconsin University Press, 1985).

Stevens, Paul, '*Paradise Lost* and the Colonial Imperative', *Milton Studies*, 34 (1996), 3–21.

Strier, Richard, 'Milton's Fetters; or, Why Eden is Better than Heaven', *Milton Studies*, 38 (2000), 169–97.

Swaim, Kathleen M., *Before and After the Fall: Contrasting Modes in* Paradise Lost (Amherst, MA: Massachusetts University Press, 1986).

Teskey, Gordon, *Delirious Milton: The Fate of the Poet in Modernity* (Cambridge, MA: Harvard University Press, 2006).

Triep, Mindele Anne, *Allegorical Poetics and the Epic: The Renaissance*

Tradition to Paradise Lost (Lexington, KY: Kentucky University Press, 1994).

* Turner, James Grantham, *One Flesh: Paradisal Marriage and Sexual Relations in the Age of Milton* (Oxford: Clarendon Press, 1987).

Webber, Joan M., *Milton and His Epic Tradition* (Seattle: Washington University Press, 1979).

Wittreich, Joseph, *Visionary Poetics: Milton's Tradition and His Legacy* (San Marino, CA: Huntington Library, 1979).

Index